STUD

FOR

LETTERS
TO
YOUNG
BLACK
MEN

STUDY GUIDE

FOR

LETTERS TO YOUNG BLACK MEN

DANIEL WHYTE III

with

Jamie McCallum & Charles Garrett

LETTERS TO YOUNG BLACK MEN STUDY GUIDE

Cover Design by Bill Hopper of Hopper Graphics.

© Copyright 2006
TORCH LEGACY PUBLICATIONS, DALLAS, TEXAS;
ATLANTA, GEORGIA; BROOKLYN, NEW YORK

First Printing, 2006

The Bible quotations in this volume are from the King James Version of the Bible.

The name TORCH LEGACY PUBLICATIONS and its logo are registered as a trademark in the U.S. patent office.

ISBN: 0-9785333-9-9

Printed in the USA.

This book is lovingly dedicated to my

Dad,

Daniel White Jr.,

My brothers:

Anthony Martin & Mark A.White,

My sons:

Daniel IV, Duran and Danyel,

My Daughters:

Daniella, Danita, Danielle, Danae`, Daniqua and Danyelle,

who I hope will find good young black men, if that is

God's will for their lives,

And to

All young black men across America and

around the world.

LETTERS TO YOUNG BLACK MEN
STUDY GUIDE
CONTENTS

PART III: ON YOUR LIFE — AS A YOUNG BLACK MAN

*Please note that the following chapters of the *Letters to Young Black Men* text are combined in the Study Guide for *Letters to Young Black Men*:

1. Letters Eight and Nine are combined in Study Eight
2. Letters Ten and Eleven are combined in Study Nine
3. Letters Twelve and Fourteen are combined in Study Ten
4. Letters Seventeen and Eighteen are combined in Study Fourteen

ACKNOWLEDGMENTS

Above all, I wish to thank God for allowing me the privilege to do such a work as this. I also wish to thank all of the pastors and youth leaders who read the book, *Letters to Young Black Men* and who decided to turn it into "curriculum" for the young men of their churches.

A very special thank you goes to Jamie McCallum for doing a magnificent job in writing most of this Study Guide, and for her sweet spirit and faithful hard work; Charles Garrett for giving me the initial idea to make a study guide out of this little book so that it could be used as a teaching and evangelistic tool in Bible studies and Sunday schools across the nation, and for his stedfast support; Bill Hopper of Hopper Graphics for designing the beautiful cover; Pete Hoelzl, Stella Cazares, and their fine staff for always doing a great job in printing our books; my daughter, Daniella, for formatting and editing this book; my wife, Meriqua, and my son, Daniel IV, for proofreading the book and for helping in the editing process; and to my youngest children, Danita, Danae`, Daniqua, Danyel Ezekiel and Danyelle Elizabeth for being obedient, quiet and patient while this book was being put together.

May God grant the increase, and receive all of the glory!

LETTERS TO YOUNG BLACK MEN STUDY GUIDE

INTRODUCTION

When I wrote the book, *Letters to Young Black Men* some time back, I never thought the book would have the kind of impact that it is having. I am thankful to the Lord for how He has chosen to use this little book. I certainly did not think that this book would be expanded into a Study Guide to be taught in small groups and churches across the nation. I am amazed at what God has done. We have received many e-mails and phone calls from people across the nation who have shared with us how the book has not only touched their lives, but changed their lives. I am very humbled by these reports.

As I said, I never thought of the book, *Letters to Young Black Men*, being expanded into a Study Guide, but since its original release, we have had many pastors to tell us that they are using the book to teach and train their young men. One pastor said that the book has become "curriculum" in his church.

I shared this with some of my close friends and advisors in the ministry, and they told me that a study guide would be perfect for Sunday schools and young men's Bible study groups. Through this advice, the Lord gave me liberty to do this Study Guide.

Born out of the requests of many from around the nation, the *Letters to Young Black Men Study Guide* was written in such a way that several men can get together and discuss it, or a young man can do it by himself. The answers are included in the back so that you can check your work and your understanding of the life principles laid down in the book, ***Letters to Young Black Men***.

I pray that it would bless your heart and help you along the success journey.

—Daniel Whyte III

Quotes from *Letters to Young Black Men*

NEVER
UNDERESTIMATE A
YOUNG BLACK
MAN

—Daniel Whyte III

NEVER GIVE UP ON A
YOUNG BLACK MAN —
BECAUSE YOU NEVER
KNOW...

—Daniel Whyte III

TO OLDER BLACK MEN:
NEVER AGAIN FORGET
ABOUT, CAST ASIDE,
NEGLECT OR MISTREAT A
YOUNG BLACK MAN, FOR
THEY WILL GROW OLDER
AND REMEMBER YOU

—Daniel Whyte III

IF YOU CONSIDER
YOURSELF YOUNG, SIR,
THEN YOU ARE YOUNG

—Daniel Whyte III

PART 1

ON YOUR LIFE –
SPIRITUAL

THE MAIN THING

STUDY ONE

"He who provides for this life, but takes no care for eternity, is wise for a moment, but a fool forever."

—Tillotson

1. You are not a _____ with a spirit.

Rather, you are a _____ with a body.

Though the physical body dies, the spirit remains.

CHECK IT OUT

Read these verses and note what they say about man's spirit:

2. Proverbs 20:27a: _____

_____

_____

3. Ecclesiastes 12:7: _____

_____

_____

4. Matthew 10:28: _____

_____

_____

_____

5. John 4:24: _____

_____

_____

6. 2 Corinthians 4:16: _____

_____

_____

7. If this last verse (2 Cor. 4:16) is correct when it says that our physical body becomes weaker, while our spirit is constantly strengthened — through increased faith, knowledge, and wisdom, then why do we spend so much time worrying about our physical health rather than our spiritual health? In other words, why do we worry so much about our physical appearance, social status, reputation, etc., and worry so little about prayer, reading the Bible, attending church, and growing in our faith?

_____

_____

_____

8. Your spiritual life, your _____
_____, should be your number one priority in this life.

9. No, it is not your _____, your _____, or even your _____.

Read these verses and note what they say about the relationship between our physical health and our spiritual life:

10. I Timothy 4:8-9: _____

_____

_____

11. I Corinthians 6:19-20: _____

_____

_____

12. So, how do we balance our desire to remain healthy with our desire to be godly?

_____

_____

_____

Read these verses and note what they say about the relationship between wealth and spirituality:

13. Proverbs 11:4: _____

_____

_____

14. Matthew 6:19-21: _____

_____

_____

15. So, according to these verses why is your spiritual life much more valuable than wealth?

_____

_____

_____

16. How does the world determine who is successful? How does God determine who is successful? Who would you rather please?

_____

_____

_____

Finally, read these verses and note the relationship between education and spirituality:

17. Proverbs 2:6: _____

_____

_____

18. 2 Peter 3:18: _____

_____

_____

19. In which ways can pursuing higher education positively contribute to our spiritual lives?

_____

_____

_____

JUST DO IT

Take some time to reflect on your spiritual life. Do you strive for health, wealth, or education more than you strive for godliness? In which areas of your life are you living to please this world more than God (i.e. in which areas are you placing more emphasis on your physical existence than your spiritual existence)? Write a letter to God asking for His help and guidance, so that you may begin to focus on your life's eternal significance. After you finish writing your letter to God, pray your letter to God.

GET TO KNOW YOUR CREATOR

STUDY TWO

"I am ready to die, not because I have lived as well as I should have; I am ready to die because Jesus lived and died so well for me."

—Daniel Whyte III

I. When I say get to know God I am talking about getting to know God _____ for _____.

a. The first step in knowing God personally is to understand that you are a _____.

b. Read 1 John 5:17. What does this verse label as sin? *"All _____."*

CHECK IT OUT

Read the following verses and note what each says about man's relation to sin:

c. Romans 3:23: _____

_____

_____

John 1:14 says that when the Word, or Jesus, came to this earth man finally experienced the glory that only comes from God. This glory is full of grace and truth. Thus, when Romans 3:23 says that every person has *"come short of the glory of God,"* it may as well be saying that every man, in his sinful state, is unworthy of God's grace and truth. Without these we are all eternally doomed.

Read the following verses and note what they say about sin:

d. James 2:10: _____

_____

_____

e. 1 John 1:8: _____

_____

_____

f. John 8:34: _____

_____

_____

We acknowledge that we are all sinners. In other words, we admit that we have let God down in the past and we continue to let Him down every day. So, the real question is, what are the consequences of my sin? If every man sins, then does God just expect such failure from human beings and, thus ignore it to some extent? Think about these questions as you work through the following section.

II. God wants us to understand that because of our _____, there is a great _____, and that punishment is _____ — both _____ death and _____ death.

Read these verses and note what they say about the effect of sin:

24

a. Psalm 5:4-5: _____

_____

_____

b. 1 Corinthians 6:9a: _____

_____

_____

c. James 1:15: _____

_____

_____

From these verses we obviously get the impression that God does not take sin lightly. In fact, He is incapable of even looking at sin because it is so repulsive. Thus, anyone who dies physically without ever having worked out this major issue between himself and the Father is sadly going to miss out on the gift of Heaven.

> **Just a thought:** Since our physical death is inevitable, while our spiritual death is avoidable, why do we spend so much of our time and energy focused on this earthly existence, and so little on knowing the Father who offers eternal life, peace, joy, and worship?

III. What are we to do about this depressing situation?

a. God wants us to understand that He _____ us more than we love _____.

b. What does Romans 5:7-8 say about the depth of God's love for you?

25

_____

_____

_____

God knew the very worst sin we would ever commit. He knew that even though we tried to put on a good face on the outside that we constantly would struggle with our thoughts and emotions. God knew we would bow down to the false idols of this world. God knew that no matter how much of Himself He gave, people would still take His name in vain, would still deny His existence, and would still live their entire lives without ever acknowledging His presence. However, He also knew that some would love Him. He knew that some would seek to honor Him with their lives, that some would be so overwhelmed by the grace shown through the life, death, and resurrection of Jesus Christ that they would seek to make His existence known to the ends of the earth. God knew that some would love Him so much that they would hunger and thirst for His presence to be known in their lives every day.

IV. In order to really know God, you must go through

_____.

Read the following verses and note what they say about the significance of Jesus Christ in the process of being forgiven for our sins.

a. Matthew 1:21: _____

_____

_____

_____

26

b. Acts 4:12: _____

_____

_____

c. 1 John 5:11: _____

_____

_____

When Jesus came to this earth as a tiny baby, God's children were anticipating a Messiah. They longed for someone to save them from oppression and to reveal the Way of the Father. Even today people are searching for someone or something to deliver them from meaningless, dead-end lives. Jesus was the answer 2000 years ago, and He still is the answer today.

V. If you want to know God, the source of all _____,
_____, _____, real _____, and
true _____, believe in your _____ that Jesus
Christ _____, was _____, and
_____ again for _____.

Ask Him to come into your heart and save you. And He will.

Are you certain that if you died today, you would experience physical death, BUT your spirit would live in Heaven with God for eternity? If so, how great it is to remember the depths of despair that the Lord Jesus saved us from! If not, then would you ask God to forgive you of your sins? Would you acknowledge that Jesus really did come to this earth to save the lost, including you? Would you ask Him to come into your heart and save you this very moment? The Bible says *"for whosoever shall call upon the name of the Lord shall be saved"* (Romans 10:13).

JUST DO IT

If you believe in your heart right now that Jesus Christ died on the cross for your sins, was buried, and was resurrected from the dead, please pray a prayer similar to this:

Heavenly Father, I realize that I am a sinner. For Jesus Christ sake, please forgive me of my sins. I now believe with all of my heart that Jesus Christ died, was buried, and rose again. Lord Jesus, please come into my heart and save my soul and change my life. Amen.

Take a moment to write a note to a friend, telling them how Jesus Christ has changed your life.

HOW TO OBTAIN THE BLESSINGS OF GOD

STUDY THREE

"Every work of God can be traced to some kneeling form."
—D. L. Moody

1. Those who are genuinely _____ and _____ in this life are those who have been _____ by God.

2. After reading the definitions of *blessing*, describe in your own words what it means to be blessed:

_____

_____

_____

It is clear that the blessings of God are integral in attaining true happiness and prosperity. So, what can you do to obtain these blessings?

3. First of all, we must have the right _____ toward our _____.

CHECK IT OUT

Read these verses and note what they say about children's relationship to their parents:

4. Proverbs 1:8-9: _____

_____

_____

5. Colossians 3:20: _____

_____

_____

6. Ephesians 6:1-3: _____

_____

_____

If you are unwilling to treat your earthly guardians with the dignity they deserve, then how can you ever expect to be able to treat the Heavenly Father with the immense submission and affection He is due? The Bible says that he who is faithful in small things will be trusted with greater things. If you fail to relate to your parents in a respectful, obedient manner, it is quite likely that you will interact with God in the same way. Thus, you will miss out on the opportunity to do great things for His name. For, He will not call a child who unashamedly harms His holy reputation. So, it seems that the real question has to do with whether or not you are seeking to live for yourself or for your Heavenly Father. If you are living for Him, it will be evidenced by a life of inherent respect and submission to others. It is in this ability to be God-minded and not self-minded that true freedom is discovered.

7. Second, in order to receive God's _____ upon your life, you must _____ to live a life that is _____ to God's Word.

8. God blesses _____, and He does _____ bless _____. He _____ has and He _____ will.

Read the following verses and note what they say about obedience:

9. Luke 6:46-49: _____

_____

_____

10. John 14:15: _____

_____

_____

11. I John 2:3-6: _____

_____

_____

Obedience basically boils down to who you are going to live for. If you choose to live for yourself, you will inevitably pursue interests that lead to instant gratification and eternal insignificance. If you choose to live for God, you will inherently desire to obey His commands, for His mercy endures forever. If you make no conscious choice considering who will receive your devotion, then you have chosen to live for yourself. Following God does not happen by accident. It is a choice you must make today, tomorrow, and every single day you are alive. In the end, it is the only decision that will affect you for eternity.

12. Third, we must spend quality time in _____ if we want God's _____ on our lives.

Read these verses and note what they say about the role of prayer in a believer's life:

13. Philippians 4:6: _____
_____
_____

14. Hebrews 4:16: _____
_____
_____

15. James 5:16: _____
_____
_____

Practice spending some time in prayer over the next few weeks. Find a quiet place and enjoy being alone with God. Spend some time praising Him for who He is — the Holy, perfect Creator of this world, the One who provides life, salvation, and purpose. Then, thank God for the many ways He has already blessed you. Too often we take God's gifts for granted, thinking we deserve them.

Next, confess your sins to God. He wants to forgive you and make you clean, but will not until you are man enough to admit you are not perfect.

Finally, share the burdens of your heart with the Father. He loves you dearly and wants to share your deepest emotions with you. For many individuals, it is quite intimidating to be this open with anyone, especially with God. However, when we are weak, He is strong. Thus, when He is strong IN us, we have the Power that created the universe working with our seemingly insignificant, finite selves to impact this world in an unbelievable way!

16. Fourth, if we want to be _____, we must have _____ in God.

17. According to Hebrews 11:1 what is faith?

_____

_____

_____

Read the following verses and note what they say about faith.

18. Psalm 118:8: _____

_____

_____

19. Jeremiah 17:7-8: _____

_____

_____

20. II Timothy 4:7-8: _____

_____

_____

21. For a _____ faith, for a more _____ faith, spend some quality time each day _____ _____

_____.

22. Last, let me encourage you to get into the habit of
_____.

Read the following verses and note what they say about giving.

23. II Corinthians 9:6-7: _____

_____

_____

24. I John 3:17-18: _____

_____

_____

Jesus, the King of the universe, did not come to be served but to serve. How much more should we adopt this vision and allow our lives to reflect such compassion! Sure it will be inconvenient, and it might even cost you a little something. But, in the end you will have gained the blessings of God, and for that there is no earthly reimbursement that even comes close to comparable.

Just Do It

25. Make a final list of the 5 ways to attain the blessings of God.

A. _____

B. _____

C. _____

D. _____

E. _____

Which of these do you need to commit to the Lord? Will you make the conscious decision today to strive for a life that is worthy of the blessings of God?

YOUR ROAD MAP TO REAL AND LASTING SUCCESS

STUDY FOUR

"Nobody ever outgrows Scripture; the book widens and deepens with our years."

—C. H. Spurgeon

1. If you desire to be truly _____ in life, you will need to _____, _____ upon and _____ the _____, and God promises good _____.

2. Do you want genuine, lasting _____? If you do, you will have to make _____ _____ a vital part of your _____ life. Your doing so will guarantee success.

CHECK IT OUT

Read the following passages and note the relationship between truly living God's Word and leading a successful life.

3. Deuteronomy 17:18-20: _____

_____

_____

4. Philippians 4:8-9: _____

_____

_____

Are you convinced that God highly esteems His Word and expects us to uphold it with absolute reverence? The Bible is not just another book. It is the very Word of God, meant to display His redemptive purposes for all of creation, for all of time. In Genesis, God breathed life into the first man, and in II Timothy, Paul claims that Scripture is God-breathed. Just as the literal breath of God gave physical life to mankind, His inspired breath, the Bible, provides spiritual life for man as well. Thus, no matter how successful you may be in the eyes of this world, if the Word is not hidden in your heart you will be far from reaching your maximum potential. We are not on this earth to merely create personal goals and achieve them. Rather, we exist to bring glory to the Father, and this is only possible if we know Him intimately. The purpose of knowing the God of the universe, the God that thought of you before there was time, is the intention of the Bible. Do you desire to know Him more intimately?

5. If so, let us look together at three suggestions for reading the Bible effectively.

    a. _____, then Read. _____ and reading the Bible go hand in hand. For you see, the Bible is a _____ book, and it will take the _____ _____ of God to teach it to you.

Read the following passages and note what they say about the spiritual nature of the Bible:

6. Luke 24:45: _____

_____

_____

7. 1 Corinthians 2:9-11: _____

_____

_____

When we lack a passion for reading and studying the Bible we
are inherently demonstrating a shallow passion for God. We must
pray that the Spirit already inside of us will actively assist our
study of the Scriptures. A true understanding of the Bible's depth
will not come without much passion and dedication. The mysteries
of the all-powerful God are not available for lightweight believers.

    b.   Read and _____ so that you can
          _____ upon what you read. To meditate means
    to _____ _____, and you cannot think
    upon something you can't _____.

Read the following verses and note why it is crucial to retain, or
meditate upon, the Word of God.

8. Matthew 4:4: _____

_____

_____

9. James 1:22-24: _____

_____

_____

    c. Read and _____. Don't just be a _____
    of God's Word, but a _____ as well.

Read the following verses and note what they say about obeying God's Word.

10. 2 Timothy 2:15: _____

_____

_____

11. Titus 1:16a: _____

_____

_____

Let us pray through the reading of Scripture. Let us meditate upon and retain the passages we study. But, let us not settle with step two. Let us press on, and actually win this race, which is the Christian life, by making our actions reflect our knowledge, and our knowledge reflect our commitment to Bible study. In this commitment, one finds true success, for he becomes more like Christ, who is truly the only individual to ever UNFAILINGLY succeed in accomplishing His purpose on earth.

12. Before concluding, list two of the five mentioned benefits to reading and meditating upon the Bible that mean the most to you.

A. _____

_____

B. _____

_____

JUST DO IT

Take some time to praise God for the gift of the Bible. Acknowledge that He was not obligated to reveal Himself to us, but He chose to, out of love and a desire to relate to us intimately.

13. Think about the place the Bible has had in your life thus far. Check the line that best describes your situation:

    _____ I have never read the Bible

    _____ I have read the Bible a few times

    _____ I only read the Bible at church

    _____ I try to read the Bible several times a week

    _____ Bible reading is a top priority in my life. I do it every chance I get.

Pray that the Lord would help you advance to this final step in which you possess a true hunger and thirst for the Word of God. Do not be intimidated if you are only on step one or two. You must start somewhere. Remember that the Holy Spirit, the only One who understands the heart of the Father, dwells inside of you.

Next, make a realistic goal related to what you will intentionally do to hide the Word of God in your heart. This may entail memorizing one verse a week, setting aside 15-30 minutes a day for true Bible study, etc. Pray that the Lord would give you strength to attain your goals.

Then, look at your life objectively, and honestly ask yourself if you are practicing what you preach. If you claim to love God, does your life display a love for your neighbor? If you say Jesus

41

is your role model, do you live a life of humility and service? If you would name Paul as your favorite Bible character, does your life also reflect a boldness and passion for taking the saving message of the Gospel to the ends of the earth? Write a prayer of confession for the times you have been lukewarm — claiming to cherish the message of the Bible, yet living for yourself. Finally, pray a prayer of renewed dedication to not merely hear the Word of God but to obey it as well.

My friend, if you have done these things you are well on your way to living an incredibly successful life!

TAP INTO UNLIMITED POWER

STUDY FIVE

"Prayer succeeds when all else fails."

—E. M. Bounds

In the last study we focused on highly esteeming the Word of God in your life. Please keep the lesson for letter four in mind as you read and work through this section on prayer. Bible study and prayer must go hand in hand. The Scriptures offer numerous promises regarding the power and positive effects of prayer, but these will not be applicable unless the Word of God is hidden in your heart. It is through God's Word that we first begin to capture His desires and passions, and it is prayer that molds these passions into our own.

CHECK IT OUT

1. Read John 15:7 and note the relationship between Bible study and prayer.

_____

_____

_____

So, as we look further into the power and benefits of prayer, let us keep in mind that neither of these come without the accompaniment of genuine Bible study.

2. There is great _____ through prayer to God.

43

3. You will find as you trail through life that you will need
_____, and _____ invites God to work
_____, _____, and _____ your life.

Read the following verses and note what they say about the power
that comes through prayer.

4. James 5:16: _____

_____

_____

5. Romans 10:12-13: _____

_____

_____

6. Matthew 21:21-22: _____

_____

_____

Ephesians 2:18 and 3:20 mentions having access to the Father.
Notice how 3:20 expands on the description of the power that
comes through such admittance to the Holy Throne of God.

If we have within us the means to tap into the power of the most
powerful Source in the entire universe, then why do we live such
defeated lives? Why do we live afraid of stepping out on faith
and attempting something amazing for God's glory? Why do we
experience feelings of insignificance and uselessness on a daily
basis? Why are we content with simply waking up, going to school
or work, coming home, watching television, and going to bed,
just to start the same routine again tomorrow?

Brothers, we are sitting on top of a gold mine. We truly have within us the ability to live so much greater than ourselves. If you will only commit your life to the Father and pray for His vision to be your vision, He will do things in your life that you would not have imagined even if you were told. So, the ultimate question must be, do you long for this power? Do you deeply desire to live the life God uniquely created you to live? Or, are you simply content with staying comfortable and watching each day pass away with nothing done of significance? If you choose the latter, do not be fooled. You are not simply wasting time, but you are missing out on the chance to live an incredible life.

If this is not enough incentive to devote your life to prayer, perhaps discussing the benefits of prayer will put you over the edge.

7. Look over the eight benefits of prayer mentioned in your book. List the three benefits that mean the most to you at this stage in your life.

A. _____

B. _____

C. _____

8. I can say not only in theory, but by _____ that "Prayer _____ things."

Read the following verses and briefly note some other benefits of prayer.

9. Exodus 6:5: _____

_____

_____

10. Deuteronomy 4:7: _____

_____

_____

11. II Chronicles 7:14: _____

_____

_____

12. Psalm 34:4: _____

_____

_____

13. Ephesians 6:18-19: _____

_____

_____

14. Hebrews 4:16: _____

_____

_____

15. James 1:5-6: _____

_____

_____

_____

16. I John 3:22: _____

_____

_____

We have clearly established the fact that prayer is an essential practice in the life of any Christian. So, how in the world do we pray? How can we possibly connect with God when we cannot see Him or audibly hear His voice? Prayer is a dialogue between our spirit and the Spirit of God. So, let us look at some guidelines concerning how and when to pray.

17. The book refers to **"The Lord's Prayer"** which is found in Matthew 6:9-13. This is a pattern Jesus gave when His disciples asked for a lesson in prayer. Fill in the blanks to create a guide you can use in your own prayer life.

  a. _____ God first.

  b. Put His _____ before yours.

  c. Ask for your _____ _____.

  d. Ask for _____ of sin.

  e. Ask God to keep you from _____.

  f. Give God the _____.

18. Lay _____ on your _____ and _____ before God and _____ His peace.

Read the following verses and note further instructions they give for how to pray.

19. Matthew 6:5-8: _____

_____

Prayer can be intimidating at first. It is difficult to know how to communicate with someone you cannot see. However, the good news is that God already knows what is on your heart. He merely desires to hear you intentionally share it with Him. To better understand this concept, think about someone you are very close to. If this person has had a great day you can probably read it all over their face when they walk in the door. Likewise, if they have had an awful day you know it also without them saying a word. However, in order for your relationship to remain intimate, do you not desire that they tell you exactly why they are overjoyed or completely bummed? It is the same with God. He knows when we love life and when we hate it. At the same time, though, He wants to be close to you and longs to communicate with you, heart to heart — without distractions. So, when you pray, get to the point. Don't ramble on, trying to please God with your words. What pleases Him more than anything is when His children trust Him enough to be vulnerable in the presence of the Holy Father. For, only when we are vulnerable can He work mightily within us. Only by the acknowledgment of our weakness is He able to transform it into our strength.

Notice what these verses say about prayer:

20. Philippians 4:6: _____

_____

_____

21. I Thessalonians 5:17: _____

_____

_____

JUST DO IT

In conclusion to this lesson it only seems appropriate to close this study by finding a quiet place and spending some time in prayer. I am not going to tell you what to pray, for only you and God know the desires and burdens of your heart. Spend some time talking to God as if He were your best friend. Before you know it that is exactly what He just might become.

THE ENCOURAGEMENT PLACE

STUDY SIX

"A good pastor will protect you from wolves, feed you, inspire you, and correct you."

—Blaine Bartel

1. Stay _____ to the _____.

2. If you have trusted Jesus Christ as your personal Savior, you

_____

_____.

Why?

I. Because _____ _____ you to be.

CHECK IT OUT

Read the following verses and note why God wants you to be involved in church.

A. Ephesians 2:19: _____

_____

_____

B. I Timothy 3:15: _____

_____

_____

II. Because going to church _____ will _____ and _____ your faith through the _____ and _____ of God's Word.

C. Read II Timothy 4:2 and note the relationship between preaching and increasing your faith.

_____

_____

_____

III. Because it (going to church) gives you the _____ and _____ to _____ and _____ God through hearing His Word, public prayers, singing, teaching, ushering, and helping others, etc.

Read the following verses and note what they say about the relationship between worshipping God and the church.

D. Matthew 18:20: _____

_____

_____

The Lord promises that when two or more come together for the purpose of worshipping Him, He will be present. How often do we enter church, go through the typical Sunday morning routine, mark it off the week's to-do list, and get on with our weekend? What a travesty to think that this one morning a week which is specifically set aside as a time to corporately meet with the Lord is often diminished of its divine value! The fact that the Lord is willing to be present in the midst of His sinful, unworthy children is a miracle in itself. When you go to church this week, focus on picturing Jesus Christ standing on the platform. Then, as you sing, pray, listen to the sermon, and interact with your fellow brothers and sisters, do it all for the purpose of bringing a smile to the Son of God. In reality, that is exactly what church is supposed to be about. Note what the verse says below:

E. Ephesians 3:21: _____

_____

_____

IV. It also gives you the _____ and _____ to _____ others and be exhorted yourself.

F. What is the definition of *exhort*? _____

_____

_____

Read the following passages and note what they say about encouragement within the body of Christ.

G. Romans 12:15: _____

_____

_____

H. Hebrews 10:25: _____

_____

_____

I. Now that we have determined the necessity of consistently attending a church, quickly note the five things to look for in a church.

1. _____

2. _____

In order to accurately identify these, you must be familiar with biblical teachings.

3. _____

4. _____

The core purpose of the church is to help the members know Jesus so they can go out and make Him known. Many churches have lost sight of this vision and simply exist to keep the membership comfortable and content. Be sure the church you join has a passion to reach this lost world for Christ. If you are already in a church and sense it has settled for this "sit back and relax" mentality, be the one to stand up and encourage renewed work for God's purposes.

5. _____

J. Finally, there are several suggestions concerning how you can make the most out of your experiences in the church:

1. Go with the _____ _____.
2. Go with a _____ _____.

3. Go with a _____ _____.

4. Go to _____ _____ and give Him the
   _____.

JUST DO IT

Basically, the act of attending church is an attempt to bring glory to the Father and to share in our worship of Him with fellow brothers and sisters. Contrary to popular opinion, church is not about us. It is solely about God and what He desires. Thus, when we sing praises to His name, we do so to worship the King of kings. When we listen to a sermon, we do so to learn more about the beautiful character of our Heavenly Father so that we can make Him known in this lost and hurting world. When we pray, we do so because our Lord desires an intimate relationship with His children, and personal communication is a key way to accomplish this. If you find yourself complaining about the style of music sung, the message of the sermon given, or the length of the prayer proclaimed, you may need to question who you seek to please by attending church.

PULLING OTHERS OUT OF THE FIRE

STUDY SEVEN

"AChristian must keep the faith, but not to himself."
—Jim Patrick

1. Since God has _____ you so, dear friend, He wants you, in turn, to be a _____ to others.

2. Jesus Christ once said to his disciples, "…._____ ye have _____, freely _____."

3. Think about three people in your life who are somehow enslaved by the fire. This may be the fire of drug and alcohol addiction, sexual immorality, purposelessness in life, etc. Write these names below:

_____

_____

_____

4. Now, think about three people in your life who you know would find themselves in the eternal fires of hell if they were to die today. Some of these may be the same individuals you thought of in the first scenario. Write these names down as well:

_____

_____

_____

Before we get into this lesson, let us spend some time reflecting on each person you listed. Does your heart break for their misfortune? When you consider the feelings of loneliness, fear, and meaninglessness that likely creep into their thoughts on a daily basis, do you shed a tear for them? Or, have you become desensitized to this lost and hurting world which surrounds you? Have you bought into the culture's lies that tell you no one is more important than you are, and as long as you have everything together nothing else really matters? Friend, I encourage you to truly inspect your heart today. Do not rush through this lesson just to finish it and move on with the day's agenda. For the sake of those names listed above, choose to proceed with humility and a sincere heart.

5. With the _____ and _____ you have received already, _____ can be used of _____ to help pull _____ _____ out of the fire.

6. List some ways people will NOT be pulled out of the fire below:

   a. _____

   b. _____

   c. _____

7. The main solution to the problems that we face in the black community is _____ and the _____ made plain in _____ _____.

Before looking at sharing God's plan of salvation with those caught in the fire, let us first discuss why we should even care about dying brothers and sisters.

Read the following verse and note what it says concerning the believer's responsibility to this lost and hurting world.

8. Matthew 4:19: _____

_____

_____

When the disciples chose to drop their nets and follow Christ, they consciously chose to leave the only life they had ever known. They considered Jesus worthy of their full devotion, and thus, left their family, friends, profession, and a likely comfortable lifestyle to obey Him. When you chose to follow Christ, did you allow Him to truly transform you? Are there any areas in your life that you are still prioritizing over sold-out devotion to the Lord? Though the disciples' lives were not easy by any means, they exemplified a true compassion and concern for the dying humanity that inhabited the earth. Thus, their obedience culminated in a selfless, yet bold love for the lost, which ultimately began the Christian movement that remains strong two thousand years later. What a legacy!

Notice what happens in the passage below to those who turn away from suffering humanity:

9. Matthew 25:35-40: _____

_____

_____

Imagine a mother whose son is teased and humiliated at school. This child comes home every day crying, intimidated, and broken.

The mother would give anything to remedy the situation, but she cannot go to school with her son everyday. In fact, that would probably only make matters worse. However, imagine that one of the most popular children in the school decided to reach out to the hurting boy. He ate lunch with him, picked him first for the basketball team, and told all the children how great this once rejected boy really was. Can you imagine how the excluded boy's mother would love the selfless child who purposefully raised her son from the depths of rejection? Just the mention of his name would bring joy to her heart and a smile to her face. For, he saved her son from an environment of loneliness and disappointment. How much more does the Father take pleasure in His children, who risk their own reputations and agendas to be certain that society's oppressed and down-trodden know they are incredibly significant in God's eyes! Do you long for the mention of your name to bring a smile to the face of God? If so, live a life of justice, never regarding yourself as better than any other. Note the following verses:

10. Luke 12:48: _____

_____

_____

11. Luke 15:4-7: _____

_____

_____

12. II Corinthians 5:20: _____

_____

_____

Now that we have determined why it is necessary to reach out to those in the fire, let us quickly review how to actually pull them out.

13. Before one can solve his problems of drugs, alcoholism, illicit sexual behavior, etc., he must deal with his _____ _____ — which is _____. And the only way that we can solve this problem is through _____ _____. And the way that we can help rescue our people from the fires of eternal punishment as well as the fires caused by the sin of our lives is by sharing with them what is called _____ _____ ____ _____.

14. List the four steps of the plan of salvation. I suggest you begin to memorize this process, because the Bible says to always be able to tell anyone what you believe and why. This is a simple, but adequate, way to answer other's questions.

A. _____

_____

B. _____

_____

C. _____

_____

D. _____

_____

There is nothing more meaningful in this life than investing in the lives of others.

JUST DO IT

In conclusion to this study I recommend that you spend some quality time praying for the names you listed on the first page of this lesson. Ask God to give you a true burden for their eternal souls and to accompany that burden with divine boldness and love. Pray for a chance to share the plan of salvation with each of those individuals in the next month. You will be utterly amazed by what God chooses to do when His children obediently turn from the life they are comfortable with and become *"fishers of men."*

PART 2

ON YOUR LIFE –
EDUCATIONAL

THE AWESOME VALUE OF READING
THE IMPORTANCE OF INCREASING KNOWLEDGE

STUDY EIGHT

"The classroom is a sanctuary."
—Daniel Whyte III

This lesson is going to be a little different than the first seven lessons. Rather than go through one lesson per letter, we are going to combine several lessons for the education section, and see how they all fit together. Thus, this lesson will cover two letters eight and nine, and you are therefore, encouraged to either read the two letters in one sitting, or work through this lesson in sections.

The focus of the book changes from your spiritual life in part one to your educational life in part two. Though we will be changing gears somewhat, the workbook will still have its roots in the Bible, for true knowledge and understanding only comes from the Giver of every good and perfect gift. With that said, let us investigate how education and godliness intertwine.

1. What is the main message of letter eight?

_____

_____

_____

_____

_____

_____

2. Read over the benefits of reading and record the three that mean the most to you:

A. _____

_____

B. _____

_____

C. _____

_____

3. Can you think of one more benefit of reading?

_____

_____

You may be asking what reading has to do with your educational life. The answer is — everything. Reading opens your mind to new ideas and gives you confidence to interact with your teacher and fellow students in your classroom. No matter what stage of life you are currently experiencing — high school, college, or working in the "real world," reading is absolutely crucial if you desire to live to your potential. It opens your eyes and mind to what God is doing in the world and helps you to authoritatively stand for His purposes in an enlightened, reason-based society.

While letter eight discusses the importance for reading as an attempt to increase your knowledge, letter nine discusses why knowledge is significant in the first place.

4. This matter of getting a good education, or _____

_____ _____, is extremely important.

CHECK IT OUT

Read the following verses and note what they have to say about increasing your knowledge:

5. Proverbs 24:5: _____

_____

_____

6. Proverbs 8:10: _____

_____

_____

7. Hosea 4:6: _____

_____

_____

Do you ever feel powerless and insignificant? Perhaps one of the surest ways to overcome such feelings is through increasing your knowledge and taking the educational process seriously. According to the verses above, knowledge truly is power.

Now that we have discussed the biblical significance of increasing your knowledge, let us investigate this issue according to what the book has to say.

8. List the seven recorded advantages of increasing your knowledge:

A._____

_____

_____

B. _____

_____

_____

C. _____

_____

_____

D. _____

_____

_____

E. _____

_____

_____

F. _____

_____

_____

G._____

_____

_____

9. May I kindly but firmly say to you _____ _____

_____ _____ _____

_____ _____! High school and college is not the

time to _____! School time is not a time for

_____! School is not a time for _____!

School is _____ _____!

10. Do your best in high school and get a good college education
of some sort "_____ _____ _____

_____."

JUST DO IT

11. To complete today's lesson I want you to do something a
little different. Think about the dreams you have or used to have
for your life, specifically for your profession. If there were no
barriers, what would you love to see come of your life? Make a
list of the things that come to mind.

_____

_____

_____

_____

_____

_____

So, what is holding you back from pursuing the above aspirations?
Do they seem impossible for a young man from your family, with
your educational background, or with your lack of finances? If
so, lesson ten is just what you need. Do not be discouraged.
Read on.

THE OBSTACLES TO GETTING
A GOOD EDUCATION
GRADUATING FROM COLLEGE AND
STILL IGNORANT AND UNLEARNED

STUDY NINE

"The best possible investment you can make in your future is an education. Even if you default on your student loan, nobody can repossess your diploma."

—Steven Silbiger

At the completion of letter nine you may be saying, "Well, all that education stuff is real easy to say, but you have no idea how impossible it would be for me to actually go to college." Perhaps, no one in your family has ever been to college. Maybe some of your siblings or relatives have gone, and they did so well that you were left feeling less than confident in your ability to accomplish the same. No matter how many excuses for not attaining more education may race through your head, graduating from high school and college is a possibility. For, *"if God be for us, who can be against us?"* Let us look together at several of the obstacles you may encounter while attempting to increase your knowledge:

I. The first obstacle that you will face is _____.

A. Obtaining a higher education will require of you a _____ ____ _____ and a _____ to stick and stay. In short, it will take _____.

Read the following verses and note what they say concerning self-discipline:

B. II Timothy 1:7: _____

_____

_____

C. Hebrews 12:1: _____

_____

_____

II. Your second obstacle to obtaining a higher education is the ever present lure of _____ _____ and _____.

Read the following passage and note what it says about immediate gratification.

A. Colossians 1:10-12: _____

_____

_____

Are you living as one worthy of the same inheritance of the great Christian leaders of the past? Or, are you so caught up with what you want and when you want it, that God's desires seem to be the last thing on your mind? Brother, if you truly desire to be great in the end, I suggest you make yourself humble now. Note what this verse says about this matter:

B. Hebrews 6:12: _____

_____

_____

III. Third, another obstacle that you will face will _____

_____ _____.

A. If they (your friends) are not increasing in

_____, and if they are not _____

you to do the same, then you _____ _____ _____

_____ _____ _____.

The Bible places a great deal of emphasis on the people with
whom God's children associate. Throughout the Old Testament
God warns His chosen ones not to be involved with foreigners.
He did so, not because He played favorites or loved one group
more than another, but because He knew these strangers
worshipped false gods and would defile His followers. Time and
time again we see how the Israelites ignored this command from
God, and thus, chose to follow a path of destruction and rejection.
Today it is just as important for the followers of God to choose
their companions wisely. God knows how easily we are influenced
by those we associate with, and therefore, speaks frequently on
this issue.

Let us look at a few more examples of what the Bible has to say
concerning our friendships:

B. Psalm 119:63: _____

_____

_____

C. Proverbs 12:26: _____

_____

_____

D. Proverbs 13:20: _____

_____

_____

IV. The fourth obstacle will be _____ _____ _____ _____.

A. List some of the characteristics that will accompany a student from a "why and how" college:

_____

_____

_____

Read these verses and note what advice they give about choosing the right college.

B. Hosea 14:9: _____

_____

_____

C. Jeremiah 29:11: _____

_____

_____

V. The fifth obstacle will be the _____.

A. List three of the ways to get an education that seem most applicable to your situation.

_____

_____

_____

B. Read Matthew 6:26-34 and note what it says about your financial needs as they relate to getting an education:

_____

_____

_____

C. I don't care what it takes or how much it costs, please get yourself a _____ _____. You will _____ regret it.

* * * * * * *

Before moving on from this issue of higher education, it is necessary to discuss how to get the most out of your educational experience. On that amazing day when you walk the platform and receive your diploma, you should not resemble the same person that entered the university four years earlier. The fact that unchanged individuals receive their college degrees every year is a travesty. It signifies an utter waste of time and money. So, let us briefly look at how we can avoid this pitfall.

1. How do people come out of a four-year institution of higher learning ignorant anyway? I believe it is because they go to college with the _____ _____ of what college is for. Some go with no intentions of _____ _____.

Note what the following verses have to say concerning your attitude toward learning:

A. Joshua 3:5: _____

_____

_____

B. I Corinthians 10:31: _____

_____

_____

If you see high school or college as a place to make a great reputation for yourself, a way to get the inside information on the best parties, or a way to find some really great dates, then it is likely you are seeking your own glory and not the Lord's. Please do not waste your time and money striving to make yourself great. Your existence is temporal and the Lord's is everlasting. Invest your energy in the more valuable cause.

JUST DO IT

To complete today's lesson, I encourage you to spend some time researching colleges in your area. Begin to make yourself familiar with the different options there are, and begin to brainstorm what your talents and skills seem to be. If you are already attending a university, examine your attitude toward learning. Are you using this God-ordained time in your life responsibly? Is God receiving the glory in your studies and in your relationships with your classmates and teachers? If not, pray for forgiveness and choose to change your attitude toward learning. If so, pray a prayer of thanksgiving to God for blessing you with this amazing opportunity of receiving higher education.

THE MARKS OF A TRULY EDUCATED MAN
PLEASE LEARN "YOURSELF" A LITTLE ETIQUETTE

STUDY TEN

"Do a common thing in an uncommon way."
—Booker T. Washington

This lesson will predominately focus on letter twelve, and a small reference to letter fourteen will be included in the last point.

After working through the previous lessons on getting an education and making the most of your studies, this lesson is beneficial for providing a self-check upon the completion of your degree. So, let us work through the ten mentioned marks of a truly educated man and see what the Bible has to say concerning most of these.

1. First, they have a _____ and _____ _____ and _____ for Almighty God.

a. A person who does _____ acknowledge and reverence God Almighty is not considered a _____ or _____ man. In fact, God considers him a _____.

We are going to pay the most attention to this issue of fearing the Lord, because if our lives truly exhibit this quality the other nine points will inevitably fall into place.

Read the following verse and note what it says concerning revering the Lord:

CHECK IT OUT

b. Deuteronomy 10:12: _____

_____

_____

Think about this... Imagine how you would feel if you were given the opportunity to spend a day with the president of the United States. Or, if that does not strike a chord, imagine you could have lunch with your favorite professional athlete. How would you act in the presence of such greatness? such success? such power? Would you interact with that person just like you do with your best friend? Surely not, for this individual is different — he is famous! How much greater and how much worthier of praise and admiration is our God than these mere human beings that He created! Should we not feel at least a small amount of anxiety upon entering His presence? Should we not make every possible effort to treat Him with the respect He deserves? God is not simply different, or just another famous name. He is THE Creator and Sustainer of this entire universe. He can wipe you and me off the face of this planet in a split second. Do you approach our Heavenly Father with this perspective? Or, does your relationship with Him simply involve what He can, and in fact should, do for you? Until we fear God enough to approach Him with our knees bent and our faces to the ground, we cannot rightly expect Him to do anything to lift us up. Think about it this way; if you are not down, how can you ever be lifted up?

Notice these verses:

c. Psalm 25:12-14: _____

_____

_____

d. Matthew 10:28: _____

_____

_____

e. Hebrews 12:28-29: _____

_____

_____

God is a consuming fire. Ultimately He will consume all forces of evil and all those who have not given Him the reverence He deserves. On that day, will you be ushered into the unshakable kingdom, or will you be consumed by the long ignored and belittled fire? A truly educated man realizes his education is absolutely worthless if it is not accompanied by a healthy fear of the Lord. Please do not waste your time and money. If you pursue higher education accompany that with an even more diligent pursuit of the Lord.

2. Second, another mark of an educated man is that he is

_____ _____ _____ _____

_____ _____.

Read the following verses and note what they say concerning humility:

a. Proverbs 22:4: _____

_____

_____

b. Matthew 23:12: _____

_____

_____

c. John 13:14: _____

_____

_____

Even Jesus Christ did not regard Himself as too important to get on his knees and serve others. This is the God and Creator of the universe bent over, washing the dirty feet of those He created! Shame on us for ever considering ourselves as above certain tasks or too important to associate with particular people. If Jesus was willing to "dirty" himself by interacting with us, we have no excuse for not doing whatever it takes to serve those He places in our lives. Any reason we find for avoiding such tasks is simply a manifestation of pride, and if there is one trait that God cannot stand it is most certainly — pride. Thus, an educated man will not use his knowledge as a way to further separate himself from those who are "below" him. Rather, he will use the skills that he attained in his pursuit of higher education to make a true difference in this world. Lasting change will only occur when the educated individual resolves to live humbly and interact with those who long for change at the very most, that is those who are currently living in discomfort and hopelessness.

3. Third, a truly educated man _____ his _____ long after his years in high school and college.

a. "He _____ until he _____."

I left college with far more questions than answers. Education was never designed to give you all of the answers to life's problems. Rather, its purpose is to help you know how to think critically, for yourself, and thus, successfully tackle any question or issue that comes your way. Once equipped with these tools, learning no longer seems intimidating or dull. Instead, it becomes your passport to destinations and experiences you never would have dreamed possible.

4. Another mark of an educated man is that he is _____.

a. List come characteristics of an authentic man:

_____

_____

_____

Read the following verses and note what they say about living authentically.

b. Proverbs 21:3: _____

_____

_____

_____

c. Revelation 3:16: _____

_____

_____

Figure out who you are and what you stand for, and live accordingly. Do not claim to follow Christ among your peers at church, and then be too intimidated or ashamed to proclaim His name at work or school. Individuals who claim to be Christians but live for themselves, actually bring more harm than good to the Kingdom of God. They cause the world to look upon believers as uncommitted, unserious, and unchanged human beings, and thus see no need to get on board. Friend, if you are not willing to boldly make a claim for Christ, please do not make any claim at all. The truly educated man is not ashamed or intimidated by the truth. Rather, he longs to invite this lost and hurting world into the arms of a healing, saving Lord.

5. Another mark of an educated man is that he uses his education and knowledge for _____ and _____ _____.

Read the following verses and note what they add to this point.

a. Luke 10:30-37: _____

_____

_____

b. II Corinthians 8:1-4: _____

_____

_____

A truly educated man will not simply hoard the products of his education, but rather will intentionally look for ways in which he can impact the Kingdom. These will include providing assistance for both the needy and the saints.

6. Sixth, one of the greatest marks of an educated man is the

_____ ____ _____ _____

_____ _____ ____ _____

_____ _____ _____ _____.

We do not need to go into more detail on this point. I believe it is self-explanatory.

7. Then, an educated man is a _____ man.

a. A disciplined man is willing and ready to tackle the difficult jobs and tasks even _____ ____ _____ _____

_____ _____ _____ _____.

Read the following verses and note what they say about self-discipline.

b. Proverbs 23:23: _____

_____

_____

c. I Timothy 4:7: _____

_____

_____

A truly educated individual realizes that life is not always going to be fun and easy, but that true growth and accomplishment comes from overcoming obstacles. Do not settle for the shallow life. Seek depth and be willing to deal with the "dirty stuff". Only then, will you truly be able to appreciate the good.

8. Eighth, the educated man exudes an inexplicable _____ _____ about himself.

What do the following verses say about the source of this confidence?

a. Psalm 27:3-4: _____

_____

_____

b. I John 2:28: _____

_____

_____

The truly educated man knows that this life does not end here on earth. He realizes that we are living for much greater purposes, and thus, he lives with an eternal mindset. He does not get carried away with making a huge salary, having a high social status, or attaining much power. Rather, he attempts to know Christ better and make Him known, for time is limited. So, when the Lord returns, as He has promised He will, there is no need for the wise believer to worry. His eternity is sealed, and his life was not wasted on temporal efforts.

9. Ninth, the educated man is not a perfect man, but he _____ to be a _____ _____.

a. It is his aim to do the _____ _____.

What do the following verses add to this point?

b. Psalm 5:12: _____

_____

_____

c. Matthew 5:20: _____

_____

_____

10. Finally, another mark of an educated man is that he understands _____ and _____.

* * * * * * *

Turn to letter 14 for the remainder of this lesson.

a. One should not only be smart in his head, but one should be smart in how he _____ _____ _____

_____.

b. After reading the definitions of etiquette, define it in your own words.

_____

_____

85

c. My definition of etiquette is _____ that which is

_____, _____, _____, and

_____ in dealing with our _____ _____

_____.

JUST DO IT

This has been an unusually long lesson, so I will not ask you to do a final exercise. Please make yourself aware of these ten marks, and as you go through your education make sure each is developing. It is truly a travesty to finish four years of higher education and suddenly realize you did not grow in any way. Make a commitment to be a smarter, stronger individual so that the Lord may use you for greater purposes.

WITH ALL THY GETTING, GET WISDOM & UNDERSTANDING

STUDY ELEVEN

"The world belongs to the man who is wise enough to change his mind in the presence of facts."

—Roy L. Smith

1. There is something more important than gaining more education and acquiring knowledge, and that is obtaining _____.

2. How does the book define wisdom?

_____

_____

_____

The dictionary lists a number of characteristics that pertain to wisdom. These include accumulated learning, the ability to discern inner qualities and relationships, good sense, and the ability to judge what is true, right, or lasting.

These definitions of wisdom make it seem like an incredibly helpful tool to possess in this world of deceptions and distractions. Let us look at several of the many biblical passages that describe wisdom.

CHECK IT OUT

3. Read the following verses and briefly note how they describe wisdom. This task may seem overwhelming due to the number of verses provided, but it is helpful for understanding the high

87

value the Bible places on attaining wisdom. At the summation of this exercise you will be equipped to create your own biblical definition of wisdom. Pay special attention to those verses marked with an asterisk.

*a. Proverbs 3:13-15: _____

_____

_____

b. Proverbs 3:18: _____

_____

_____

*c. Proverbs 4:6-7: _____

_____

_____

d. Proverbs 8:12: _____

_____

_____

*e. Proverbs 9:10: _____

_____

_____

f. Proverbs 23:4: _____

_____

_____

*g. Proverbs 28:26: _____

_____

_____

h. Ecclesiastes 7:11: _____

_____

_____

*i. James 3:17: This verse gives a great list of the characteristics which define wisdom. List each of these below.

1. _____

2. _____

3. _____

4. _____

5. _____

6. _____

7. _____

8. _____

4. Here is just a mini quiz to make sure you caught the main component of wisdom. According to what you have just read, what is the beginning of all wisdom? (If you need help, re-read Proverbs 9:10).

_____

5. Now combine all that we have done to this point and create your own definition of wisdom. It does not have to be fancy or sound like it is straight out of the dictionary. Rather, simply write a sentence or two describing what you have decided the term *wisdom* signifies:

_____

_____

_____

Now that you have a good understanding of what wisdom is, let us investigate how it can be acquired.

6. According to the book, the basic way to obtain true wisdom is to _____ _____ _____ _____!

7. You cannot _____ for wisdom, you cannot _____ and get wisdom, you cannot _____ wisdom, you cannot _____ wisdom, and you cannot _____ wisdom from other human beings.

Asking God for wisdom is certainly the key to its attainment. The following verses give some insight into how to appropriately approach the throne of grace when requesting such a gift.

Read these passages and note what they add to James 1:5.

a. Proverbs 1:7: _____

_____

_____

b. Proverbs 2:1-5: _____

_____

_____

c. Proverbs 8:17: _____

_____

_____

To be wise is to know the ways of Christ, love the ways of Christ, and ultimately follow in the ways of Christ.

d. Proverbs 11:2: _____

_____

_____

When asking God for wisdom, be assured that He knows your heart. If you desire to be wise in order to stand apart from your peers and, thus, receive personal attention than you are wasting your time and energy. He will not honor your request. However, if you truly desire wisdom so that you may be a more useful servant of Jesus Christ, have faith that He will honor such a humble petition.

e. Matthew 7:24: _____

_____

_____

8. Finally, if you want to be wise, it is wise to _____ or _____ with _____ _____. If you hang with fools, you will eventually become a _____ _____.

Read the following verse and note what it says about your choice in friends:

a. Proverbs 12:26: _____

_____

_____

To be wise you must be aware of the things and people that tend to influence you. Whether you see it or not, the friends you spend the most time with will always affect the way you think, talk, and act. Thus, it is crucial that you are extremely cautious in choosing who or what will fill your time. If you hang out with an individual who is seeking after the things of this world, it is likely that you will soon find yourself possessing the same priorities and dead-end goals. However, if you wisely choose companions that love the Lord and deeply desire to know Him more, your own hunger and thirst for godly things will grow. In the end, your life will be full of opportunities to make a positive difference, and you will be richly blessed.

In conclusion to today's lesson review the characteristics of wisdom. Do you truly desire to be wise, or are you content with coasting through life, never really challenging yourself to live to your potential? If you can honestly say you prefer the wisdom route, review the process of attaining it. Is this possession of wisdom important enough for you to fear God, prize His Word, strive daily to be more like Christ, and humble yourself continuously?

JUST DO IT

If so, take a moment to intentionally ask God for wisdom. When approaching Him with a humble and pure heart you can rest assured that your request will be met. However, do not end with that. Rise up from your prayer with a new found commitment to walk in the way of the wise. This path has no room for ungodly friends, but those who love the Lord make for great company. If you remain on this narrow path, your life will surely stand apart from most everyone you know. In the end, you will know your Father with an intimacy you never imagined possible.

PART 3

ON YOUR LIFE – AS A YOUNG BLACK MAN

YOU ARE NOT INFERIOR!

STUDY TWELVE

"I did not equate my self-worth with my wins and losses."
—Arthur Ashe

We are going to do this lesson a little differently. The book lists several reasons why many young black men feel inferior in today's world. We will quickly review these points, and then examine why the Bible says no Christian should ever feel insignificant or defeated in the world. In other words, the book tells you why you might feel inferior to other races, and this lesson will tell you why you should not.

First, use your book to determine some of the ways the "disease" of inferiority is contracted.

1. One way to get this disease is by _____ being _____ _____.

a. Young black children need lots of _____, _____, and _____ to turn out right in this strange society that we live in, especially _____ _____. It is _____.

Have there been influential people in your life who have displayed these qualities (parent, grandparent, teacher, coach, etc.)? If so, list his or her name and take some time to thank God for that person. If not, be aware that you may be extra vulnerable to this inferiority complex disease. But, ONLY be aware. Do not use

97

this as an excuse for your feelings and, thus, your actions.

_____

_____

2. The second reason why young black men feel inferior to others is because they have become _____ to that one eyed monster- the _____ _____.

a. This happens simply because those who grow up with a heavy diet of television watching are constantly watching _____ on the tube _____ things and who are _____ and _____ _____ with their lives while they just _____.

b. Circle the option below that best describes your daily habits.

I watch television:

> (A) Less than 7 hours a week
> (B) More than 7 and less than 15 hours a week
> (C) More than 15 hours a week

The time I take to read my Bible, pray, and attend church events is:

> (A)   Less than 5 hours a week
> (B)   More than 5 hours a week, but less than 10 hours a week
> (C)   More than 10 hours a week

Which takes up more of your time? How does that reflect your priorities?

3. A third reason for this feeling of inferiority among young black men is because many do not _____ more _____.

a. Knowledge is _____, and may I say _____ _____.

We have already discussed this issue of education, knowledge, and wisdom in depth. Thus, let us move on to reasons you should not feel inferior.

CHECK IT OUT

Read the following verses and note who they say you are in Christ.

b. Psalm 27:1-3: _____

_____

_____

c. Philippians 4:13: _____

_____

_____

Think about the dreams you had for your life when you were a child. Do you still dream in the same way? Or, has this harsh world talked you out of those "childish" things and forced you to accept some lot you never would have wished for? Friend, God promises to give you the strength to do anything you put your mind to. You must have faith in this promise and desire to glorify Him first and foremost. Then, the boundaries truly do disappear, and God can use you to accomplish things you never imagined. God is never hindered by society's prejudices. He sees into man's heart and will choose to use the humble, yet confident follower over the man that fits this world's distorted standards any day.

d. Romans 8:31: _____
_____
_____

Now that we have looked at several verses that generally describe why the believer should never feel inferior, let us look at three specific ways the Bible address those areas that typically cause young black men, and all people, to feel this way.

1. First of all, you may feel physically inferior to others.

What do the following verses say about who you physically are in Christ?

a. I Samuel 16:7: _____
_____
_____

b. Psalm 139:13-14: _____
_____
_____

c. Matthew 17:20: _____
_____

Through faith and courage you will have incredible influence in this world which is greatly lacking in true men of God. If God thought you were inferior, such power would never be offered into your hands. So, if He thinks you are worthy of such responsibility, why do you not agree?

2. Second, you may feel intellectually inferior to others.

Read the following verses and note what they say about such feelings.

a. Luke 21:15: _____

_____

_____

b. I Corinthians 1:25-27: _____

_____

_____

You may feel as though school and studying is just not for you. Perhaps you consistently struggle with feelings of inferiority when comparing your intelligence to your siblings' or peers'. Please understand that no aspect of your character is a hindrance to God's plan. In fact, He is the one that created you with the exact intellectual capacities you possess. Allow yourself to be confident enough to be called by God. Those who He calls, He completely prepares.

3. Finally, you may feel economically inferior to others.

Perhaps you fear you will never be able to afford a college education. It could be that most of the wealthier students at your school have their own vehicles, and you have to walk to school or ride the bus. Maybe you are embarrassed to bring friends to your home because their home is much bigger and newer. Or, perhaps you are working a dead-end job and are just beginning to realize that at this rate, you will never be able to build up a savings account. Not surprisingly, the Bible also has quite a bit to say concerning finances.

Read the following verses and note how they speak to those who feel economically inferior to others:

a. Joshua 1:8: _____

_____

_____

b. Psalm 112:1-3: _____

_____

_____

c. Matthew 6:30-33: _____

_____

_____

The Lord knows exactly what you need even before you ask Him and He has every intention to fulfill these needs. Likewise, He knows it is difficult to watch as others flourish and you seem to hit one dead-end after another. Nonetheless, Jesus' words to you are "Do not worry, my child." He loves you dearly and wants the very best for you. Maybe your economic struggles now are teaching you to truly appreciate financial blessings down the road. Or, perhaps your financial situation is showing you what it means to trust in God, even when life is not easy. He will take care of you today, tomorrow, and the next day. In the end, we will all be in Heaven praising Him as complete equals.

JUST DO IT

In conclusion to today's lesson pray a prayer about your feelings of inferiority to the Lord. Boldly claim what you have in him — physical strength, the ability to influence others, intellectual prowess, and all you need to successfully make it through each day. Repent of feelings of inferiority, and ask the Lord to help you overcome those pitfalls that bring these feelings about. Praise God, for He wants to use YOU AND ONLY YOU to make an incredible difference in this world! Do not make Him choose His second choice, for he surely will not be as qualified for the task.

TAKE THE ROAD LESS TRAVELED

STUDY THIRTEEN

"When you do the things you have to do when you have to do them, the day will come when you can do the things you want to do when you want to do them."

—Zig Ziglar

1. What is the road less traveled?

_____

2. Discipline is that quality that says, by the grace of God, come hell or high water, I am _____ to get the _____ _____ or _____ that _____, etc. Discipline says it doesn't matter how I _____ or what is _____ _____ around me or who is doing or saying what. All that matters is that I am _____ to _____ to do _____ things, if necessary, to reach my goal.

We have already discussed the topic of self-discipline in several previous chapters. Thus, this lesson will simply serve to refresh your memory on areas that you, as a believer, should exercise discipline in, and give you some guidance in how to go about possessing such self-control.

3. List the five things that we really need to practice the principle of discipline in:

A. _____

B. _____

C. _____

D. _____

E. _____

4. First, let us look at the discipline of prayer.

a. You will need to learn to pray when you _____ like praying and even when you _____.

CHECK IT OUT

b. Quickly skim the following passages and note what they all have in common. You do not need to comment about each one. Just read them quickly and determine the common theme:

Matthew 14:23	Matthew 19:13
Matthew 26:36	Mark 1:35
Luke 3:21	Luke 6:12
Luke 9:28	Luke 11:1
Luke 22:39	John 17

c. Read Luke 5:16 and paraphrase what it says.

_____

_____

_____

Jesus did not only pray when He felt like it, when He was at the temple, or when He encountered a crisis. Rather, Jesus regularly took himself to a solitary location and spent time with the Father. I do not doubt that there were many times Jesus was exhausted or had seemingly more important things on His agenda, but nonetheless He realized that spending time with the Father was imperative. He likely left such meetings energized and empowered to face the world for yet another day. If we desire to live as Christ lived, should we not adopt the same habits and priorities He possessed?

5. Secondly, you should be disciplined in reading, especially _____ reading.

a. Read Ephesians 6:10-17. In the armor of God, what article applies to the Word of God, or the Bible?

_____

b. Can you determine how the sword differs from all of the other pieces of armor? Please actually take some time to think about this question before reading on. See if you can't solve it yourself. Write your thoughts below.

_____

_____

_____

_____

_____

Answer: The sword is the only offensive piece of armor. The belt, breastplate, shield, helmet, etc. merely provide defense against the enemy's attacks. However, the sword actively attacks the enemy and seeks to intentionally take him down. The Bible says that the "devil is like a roaring lion seeking whom he may devour." Unfortunately, brother, that includes you. The enemy will do anything to see you fall and to separate you from Christ. So, rather than simply stand back and attempt to defend yourself against these attacks, why not pull out your sword and go after the devil yourself? You will never be fit for such a battle if the Word of God is not hidden in your heart. The Bible gives you everything you will ever need to live a victorious life. Begin now to devote time and energy to reading God's Word. Trust me, you will be so glad you did.

6. Next, let us see what the Bible has to say about in-depth study. It is true that mental exercise is often more difficult than physical exercise, but its results also tend to last longer. Read the following verse and note what it says about study.

a. Ecclesiastes 12:12: _____

_____

_____

b. II Timothy 2:15: _____

_____

_____

What does the amount of time you spend in God's word suggest about how much you delight in the Father?

7. The last two areas you should be disciplined in, exercise and sex, somewhat go together, because both deal with how you treat your physical body. Thus, let us look at several verses that describe how to appropriately treat yourself, for you are the temple in which the Holy Spirit dwells.

Read the following verses and note what they say about the issue of self-discipline in exercise, sex, or both:

a. Romans 12:1: _____

_____

_____

b. I Thessalonians 4:3-5: _____

_____

_____

c. I Corinthians 6:18-20: _____

_____

_____

8. Have you ever seen in a photograph or on television the huge cathedrals in Europe?

These buildings were built years ago in order to provide a place for the communal worship of Jesus Christ. When looking at these churches you automatically know they serve a very special purpose. The artwork on the walls, ceilings, and floors is the very best from that time period, the sanctuary is adorned with gold and precious ornaments, and the many pillars point straight to the Heavens. When individuals enter these places they inherently know to be silent and carry themselves in a respectful manner, for these cathedrals have purposely been designed so that all may know they are worthy of the presence of Almighty God. Now, think about yourself. You are also called to be the temple of the Holy Spirit. Do you diligently avoid all the "junk" this world throws at you, as to not defile this holy dwelling place. Is your life adorned with the most beautiful things available — love, compassion, and humility? Do your thoughts and actions clearly point away from yourself and directly to God in Heaven?

Remember, your body does not belong to you. Sure, you can choose what to eat, how often to exercise, and whether or not you will engage in sexual immorality. However, this does not make you the owner. God created you and paid a very special price — the blood of His Son, in order to keep your body pure and holy. Now, you have been given the incredibly huge responsibility of maintaining this temple in a way that glorifies the Father. Please do not make this precious gift worthless by treating your body as though its only purpose is to fulfill your immediate physical desires.

a. I Corinthians 3:16-17: _____

_____

_____

If you are watching a television show which has sexual references, have the self-discipline to turn it off. If you are listening to a song which puts inappropriate visions in your head, choose to honor God, and change the station. If your friends are talking about sex as though it is just an accepted activity with no responsibilities or obligations attached, be bold to speak up for the Lord. To say nothing is to essentially agree. In all that you do ask yourself whether or not you would be ashamed if Christ was in the room with you, for in reality HE IS.

Now that we have looked at the areas in which you most need to practice self-discipline let us quickly review how to practice this discipline. Review the seven suggestions from the book. Record the three that you think would help you most when attempting to complete a difficult task.

_____

_____

This topic of self-discipline can be overwhelming at first. You may have gone through the five areas and felt as though you were failing in each one. Please do not be discouraged. Remember in the previous lesson we looked at the verse that says, *"I can do all things through Christ which strengtheneth me."* The fact that you have made it through sixteen lessons in this workbook is an amazing accomplishment in self-discipline. Believe in yourself and allow God to make you purer and holier each day.

JUST DO IT

To wrap up this lesson choose one of the five areas in which you need to demonstrate self-discipline. Write your choice below:

_____

_____

Now, from the seven suggestions for practicing discipline, choose at least two that you will apply in your attempt to master the discipline. Write these below:

1. _____

_____

2. _____

_____

Now, pray to the Lord for strength and commitment to see this through. You will not be transformed automatically, but each day, step by step, God will honor your commitment and make you more like Christ. In several months, you might just look back and be completely astonished by what the Lord has done in your heart and mind.

TAKE FULL RESPONSIBILITY
TALK AND LISTEN TO EVERY OLDER BLACK MAN PAST FIFTY THAT YOU POSSIBLY CAN

STUDY FOURTEEN

"Truth is proper and beautiful in all times and in all places."
—Frederick Douglass

Once again we are going to combine two letters in this lesson. We will quickly review what the book has to say about taking responsibility, and then we will specifically focus on how this applies to being instructed by older, faithful men.

Let us begin by looking at letter 17.

1. Somehow, many of us, as young black men, did _____ acquire a _____ attitude towards self-_____. Frankly, many of us are _____ of responsibility. The lack of this one quality can _____ you throughout your life.

CHECK IT OUT

Read the following verse and note what it says about responsibility:

a. Ezekiel 18:20: _____

_____

_____

Friend, it is time for you to stop making excuses about factors you cannot control, and begin to make something of YOUR life. You will never be able to change others until you first focus on changing yourself. In the end, you only have one life to live and you will be accountable for what you did with that life. God is not interested in excuses. He knows exactly where you have come from and what you have been through. What makes Him proud is to see how you make the most of your past situations and glorify him regardless.

2. According to the book, what is the main reason many young black men do not have a healthy attitude towards self-responsibility?

_____

_____

a. Read Proverbs 1:5. How does this verse relate to the point above?

_____

_____

3. Think of some older black men you know who really seem to exemplify Christ and His wisdom. Perhaps this is a family member, a teacher, or pastor, or even a member of your church. List their names below:

_____

_____

_____

_____

4. If you cannot think of anyone, you must make an attempt to place yourself in the midst of such positive influences. Rather

than writing names, write places where you will attempt to encounter older, wiser black men:

_____

_____

_____

_____

Now it is up to you to take the initiative to learn from their instruction.

We will delve into this issue of instruction and mentorship with greater detail upon the completion of this study of letter 17.

5. A second reason why we do not take responsibility for our lives as we should is because _____-_____ goes _____ _____ _____.

a. It is human nature, and much _____ to be _____ than _____.

Read the following verses and note the tendency of human beings to avoid responsibility. Also, determine what the consequences of denying responsibility are in these cases.

b. Genesis 3:12-13 (If you are not familiar with the creation story you may want to read all of Genesis 3 in order to better understand this reference.): _____

_____

_____

_____

c. Exodus 32:1-28: _____

_____

_____

You may not think that your responsibilities can even compare to those of Adam and Eve or Aaron. For these people were trusted with beginning the human race and overseeing the entirety of God's chosen people. Because their responsibilities were great, the consequences of irresponsibility were even greater. For the former, every human that exists for all of time will now have to live with the ever present threat of sin. For the latter, five thousand lives were lost due to one act of disobedience. Though the consequences of your lack of self-responsibility may come on a much smaller scale, they certainly do come.

For example, if you ignore your responsibility to marry the mother of your child, then your little girl is growing up without a father to teach her about respecting her body and to tell her she is beautiful and a gift from God. Your little boy is being raised without a daddy to play catch with, to cheer him on at his football games, and to teach him how to become a respectable man. If you do not take on the responsibility of making sure you are at work during your scheduled time, then you are causing a co-worker to miss precious time with his family just so he can hold up your end of the bargain. If you are not responsible enough to take care of your body and choose to use drugs or become addicted to alcohol you are not only harming yourself but are causing those people who care about you to spend many restless nights, pleading with the Lord on your behalf.

Brother, a lack of self-responsibility has led to widespread consequences ever since the Garden of Eden. Why do you think your actions, or lack of actions, are any different?

6. List the three dangers of not taking responsibility for yourself:

A. _____

_____

B. _____

_____

C. _____

_____

7. According to the book, what is the main way you can be a completely responsible person now?

_____

_____

_____

8. Take _____ for _____ that you _____, all that you _____ and all that you _____ and never _____ anyone else for your situation.

* * * * * * *

Now that we have a good idea of the need for living a responsible life, let us look back at the idea of seeing this characteristic exemplified by older black men. Not only can these men teach you to live responsibly, but they can also instruct you in numerous areas of your life. Turn to letter 18 and fill in the blanks.

9. I suggest to you that it is very important that you spend some
_____ _____ _____ to and _____
to every _____ _____ _____ past fifty that you
possibly can.

10. List two of the four positive things that older men can impart
to those who are ready to listen:

A. _____

B. _____

Now, as we look at a biblical example of such mentorship, you
may question why we are focusing on Jesus, who clearly is not
an old man in the Bible. In reality, you are instructed to learn
from older people, because they have experienced more in life
and thus are able to bestow this wisdom upon you. Those men
that seem the most wise in your eyes are probably also the most
Christ-like. Thus, Jesus is the perfect example of a mentor, for
He is all-knowing and His "foolishness" is wiser than man's
deepest wisdom. Therefore, please do not let the age of Christ
distract you from His and the disciples' examples on mentorship.

11. Read Luke 2:46 and note what Jesus was doing in his teenage
years:

_____

_____

As a young man Jesus took advantage of His opportunity to learn
from the spiritual leaders and to ask questions. He was not
intimidated by His age or social standing. Likewise, as a young
man, you are at the perfect age for learning and asking questions.
As we see what such a focused childhood and adolescence

produced in Jesus' life, we will make comparisons to how this affects your own life today.

After this episode Jesus continued to grow and become strong, increasing in wisdom (Luke 2:40).

12. Turn to Matthew 4:18-24 and note what such responsibility and discipline prepared Him to do:

_____

_____

In order for Jesus to become a teacher He first had to be a student. In order for Him to be a leader He first had to be a follower. After years of such submission and training, the Son of God was finally ready to begin His transforming ministry.

13. Now, let us shift our focus from Jesus' role to that of the disciples. In Matthew 5:1 what do the disciples do? _____

_____

14. Now, from Matthew 5:2 to Matthew 7:29 what is happening?

_____

_____

15. Finally, skip ahead to Matthew 10:1-8. What is happening in this scene?

_____

_____

_____

_____

I hope you caught the pattern in the life of Jesus and his disciples. As a boy, Jesus was intentional about learning from old, wise teachers. He then became equipped to lead others, who He instructed in all the ways of life. After intentionally spending days, weeks, and months at Jesus' side the disciples had been instructed in the way of truth, and were thus able to go out and find their own followers.

Just Do It

Brother, if you desire to be like one of those men you listed at the bottom of page two of this study, then you must first be willing to spend time learning from such individuals. Even Jesus was not too wise, too cool, or too busy to ignore the instruction of spiritual leaders. Today, you are called to be a disciple of Jesus Christ just like the twelve were chosen two thousand years ago. Will you make the effort to diligently learn from the life of Christ and from every older, wiser individual the Lord places in your path? If so, one day you will receive the official sending out from the Father, and then your life as a spiritual leader will truly begin. Please do not forget that you must follow before you lead.

LEARN ABOUT WHERE YOU COME FROM

STUDY FIFTEEN

"Our Black heritage must be a foundation stone we can build on, not a place to withdraw to."

—Colin L. Powell

1. Learning about your heritage and where you come from is crucial to your _____-_____, _____, and vision for the _____. As they say, a person who does not know _____ _____ _____ _____ does not know _____ _____ _____ _____.

2. What are four ways you can make yourself familiar with your heritage?

    A. Take some time and _____ your _____ _____, and ask them questions about how it was "back when."

    B. It would help you greatly to read two or three _____ _____ _____ books,

    C. As well as history books on _____.

    D. And two or three general _____ _____ books.

Now, let us see what the Bible has to say about the importance of understanding your heritage. In order to do this, we are going to observe a case study of the Israelites.

The Israelites were the people to whom God first chose to reveal Himself. He loved them and made a covenant with them which said, that the Israelites would be God's people and He would be their God. He would never leave nor forsake these chosen ones as long as they did not forsake Him. This personal identity with the one and only true God set Israel apart thousands of years ago and continues in the lives of Christians, for the blood of Jesus made all believers God's chosen children. Thus, let us look at how the issue of heritage affected the Israelites back in the Old Testament times and then decipher what that means for the Christian believer today.

CHECK IT OUT

In the book of Exodus, we find the Israelites living in bondage among the Egyptians. God hears their laments and pleas for liberation, and thus, raises up His servant Moses to speak to pharaoh, Egypt's ruler, who eventually, with significant influence from God Himself, allows the Israelites to freely leave his country. Exodus 12:21-42 picks up on the night the Israelites were finally going to be freed from their oppressors. Read this passage and pay special attention to verses 24-27.

3. What event does the Passover commemorate?

_____

_____

_____

4. Why would it be significant for Israelite parents to pass on to their children the meaning of Passover? (vss. 26-27)

_____

_____

5. Now read verses 50-51 of this same chapter. How did the Lord reward the Israelites for their obedience to His commands?

_____

_____

_____

Now turn to Exodus 14. This chapter picks up on the Israelite's voyage out of Egypt. Pharaoh has suddenly had a change of heart, and worries that his country cannot exist without the workforce that was provided by the Israelites. Thus, the Egyptian army takes off after the fleeing Israelites, who soon find themselves caught between an impassable body of water, the Red Sea, and an angry army seeking their recapture.

6. Read Exodus 14:13-31. What does Moses command of the Israelites in verse 13?

_____

_____

_____

7. What happens in verses 21-22 as a result of the Israelites' obedience?

_____

_____

_____

8. What claim does the Egyptian army make in verse 25?

_____

_____

_____

9. How does the fate of the Israelites differ from that of the Egyptians as seen in verses 27-29?

_____

_____

_____

10. What do you suppose was the difference?

_____

_____

_____

After crossing the Red Sea, the Israelites roamed in the desert for many years. God wanted to make sure His children had complete faith in His covenant before He lavished the gift of the Promised Land upon them. However, even in the desert they were not alone. God provided for their physical needs every single day. In Exodus 16 we read about how the Lord provided manna and meat for His children to enjoy. For a people roaming in the desert, this is an amazing blessing.

11. Read Exodus 16:31-33. What did God command Moses and Aaron to do with the manna?

_____

_____

_____

12. Why? _____

_____

_____

_____

Now, look ahead to Exodus 17:8-14. These verses record the first battle the Israelites faced as a freed people. Read these verses and answer the questions below.

13. In verse 11, what determined whether or not the Israelites were winning the battle?

_____

_____

_____

14. What was the final outcome of the battle according to verse 13?

_____

_____

_____

15. What does the Lord command in verse 14?

_____

_____

_____

16. Are you beginning to see a pattern? The Lord continuously did remarkable, miraculous things in the presence of His children, the Israelites. He spared their children from the plague of death, He parted an entire body of water so they could cross on dry land, He led them with a cloud by day and fire by night, He provided constant meat and bread in the dry, arid desert, and He destroyed an entire army of enemies by simply raising the arms of the Israelite leader in the air. You may be telling yourself that if God worked like that in your life it would be a lot easier to believe in Him. However, the Lord did not promise such provision

and strength without a price. In Exodus 19:3-6 He makes a covenant with His followers, and tells them that such blessings will only continue under one condition. According to verse 5, what was this condition?

_____

_____

_____

_____

Unfortunately, the Israelites could not hold up their end of the bargain. Eventually, the manna and quail were no longer seen as supernatural provisions, but as tasteless expectancies. While their God might provide security and uniqueness, other gods allowed their followers to possess gold and silver and engage in sexual practices. Slowly, the Israelites stopped dwelling on all the good that God had done for them, and they began to complain about ever leaving Egypt. They desired the certainty that accompanied the land of bondage and oppression over the vulnerability of trusting God to deliver them from the inhabitants of their promised land. Thus, Numbers 14 tells the story of the Israelites rebellion against their God. The Lord had enough of their inconsistency and lack of faith.

17. According to Numbers 14:11 why is the Lord so frustrated with the Israelites?

_____

_____

_____

18. What is the punishment for the unbelief of the Israelites according to verses 20-23?

_____

_____

_____

Okay, now let us tie all of this together. God dearly loved the Israelite people and specifically called them out to be His followers. When they suffered from the chains of bondage, God heard their cries and released them. When they were in a seemingly hopeless situation, God performed a miracle and split the Red Sea in half. When they were starving in the desert God sent food from the sky, and never stopped providing such nourishment until they entered the "land flowing with milk and honey." When the Israelites found themselves tired, weary, and suddenly at war with the Amalekites, God supernaturally intervened and gave His children a hands down (no pun intended) victory. Then, as a commitment to continue anointing His children with such blessings God laid out their own personal covenant. He said, "As long as you, your children, your grandchildren, your great grandchildren, etc. continue to trust Me, I will continue to provide for you." However, somehow the Israelites let God down. They became so obsessed with their present situations that they forgot to continue telling the stories of what God had done. They turned their eyes from the words of the covenant to the false promises offered by surrounding nations. They began to dwell on their hardships instead of their blessings. They neglected their heritage and the faith of their fathers and desired the empty blessings of this world. And, thus, God remained true to His covenant and took His blessings from those He dearly loved.

Friend, this story relates more to you as a young, black Christian than you probably realize. Like the Israelites, your people have lived through extremely difficult times, and have been freed from the chains of bondage. The amazing faith of your ancestors carried them through such oppression more than any president, legislation, or civil rights movement ever could. God hears the cries of His hurting children, but when He responds and saves you from despair He expects you to remember it. Read about black heroes who boldly stood for God and fearlessly spoke against slavery. Talk to your relatives who lived during the Civil Rights movement and ask how it affected them. Do not assume that because you were not alive during such times, you are not affected by those events. The lack of faith of the Israelites significantly affected their children and grandchildren, which is seen in Israel's constant struggle to have Godly leadership and peace.

Your heritage as a Christian runs even deeper than your heritage as a black man. The Christian story begins in Genesis 1:1 and continues for eternity. These events in the lives of the Israelites are relevant to you and me, because as believers we are now God's chosen people. He miraculously saved us from the bondage of sin, and has given us a purpose for living, to bring glory to His name. In order to remember this purpose and to make the most of this covenant that we now share with the Father we must study our spiritual heritage and learn from it. We can be proud of the men and women of the faith that are highlighted in the Bible, and we can vow to learn from those who let God down. The Lord has placed you in your specific family, in this particular country for a reason.

JUST DO IT

As one of God's chosen children there is a purpose for your life. In order to make the most of it, you must first understand where you come from physically and spiritually, and then allow yourself to feel proud about those areas in your family's past that glorify

God and to learn from those areas that were contrary to His desires. Whatever you do, do not forget what the Lord has done. Remembrance is truly the key to His covenant. But, how can you ever remember His mighty works in the life of your family if you do not make yourself aware of your own heritage?

THE VALUE OF WORKING HARD AND SMART

STUDY SIXTEEN

"The secret to success is to learn to accept the impossible, to do without the indispensable, and to bear the intolerable."
—Nelson Mandela

1. Those who choose to be _____ and _____ with their lives usually end up _____ and _____ upon others; while those who make up their minds to _____ _____ end up having the things they _____, and also many of the _____ things that they _____.

Let us look at what several verses in the book of Proverbs have to say concerning laziness. Please realize that Proverbs is a book of observations rather than set in stone facts. Thus, it is probable that you know someone in your life who is the epitome of laziness and yet seems to have everything they ever wanted. Likewise, you may know others who work day in and day out and struggle just to make ends meet. Nonetheless, both scenarios are exceptions to the rule. The author of Proverbs has observed the facts of life and recorded the tendencies he noticed. These are just as applicable to the 21st century as they were thousands of years ago.

CHECK IT OUT

Read the following verses and note what they say concerning those who CHOOSE laziness.

2. Proverbs 10:5: _____

_____

_____

3. Proverbs 14:23: _____

_____

_____

4. Proverbs 18:9: _____

_____

_____

5. Proverbs 21:25: _____

_____

_____

If you choose to live a lazy life, do not complain when your peers who have pursued higher education and are working diligently seem to have everything while you have nothing. Do not cry out "Injustice", for this world has never been one that caters to those who simply expect to be catered to. Opportunity and blessings follow those whose lives are worthy of such benefits.

6. What are the three ways one becomes slothful and lazy?

A. _____

_____

B. _____

_____

C. _____

_____

7. Most of television is fiction and we cannot continue to live
_____ lives in a _____-_____ world. Get this:
_____ is not _____!

Now that you are aware of the dangers a lazy man faces, let us
look in more detail at five ways you can break the slothfulness
habit.

8. Sit down and define what you are about and what it is you
would like to _____ in life. Set _____
_____ and _____ them.

Read the following verses and note what they add to this point.

a. Proverbs 20:4: _____

_____

_____

Just like the farmer who must plow months before he receives
any fruit from his labor, you must begin to work hard now,
realizing it will take time for your dreams to become realities. If
you are not disciplined or focused enough to accept such delayed
gratification, then you are ultimately settling for the simple,
shallow life.

b. John 6:27: _____

_____

_____

c. Before moving on to the second point, take a little time to
think about what you want from your life. Fifty years from now,

what accomplishments do you hope to look back and see? List these below:

_____

_____

_____

_____

_____

_____

d. Now, choose one accomplishment and record ways you might go about achieving it:

_____

_____

_____

_____

You will likely want to come back to this exercise at a later time and spend more time determining what you want your life to be about and how you will intentionally attempt to accomplish these desires.

10. Make up a _____ _____ and _____ how you will _____ your goals. And then pursue them like a _____ _____.

How do these verses relate to this point?

a. Proverbs 10:4: _____

_____

_____

b. Proverbs 21:5: _____

_____

_____

Learn to follow your plan even when it feels as though progress is minimal. When you finally do achieve your goal, you will realize that the process was more rewarding than the goal itself.

11. Be _____ with the tenacity of a Bulldog, that you will not let _____ or _____ get in your way of doing what you _____ you _____ _____ _____.

Read the following verses and note how they contribute to this idea.

a. Proverbs 15:19: _____

_____

_____

When you decide once and for all to make something of your life, the devil will not let that decision go unnoticed. He will try all he can to tempt you to settle for mediocrity and the easy life. Keep your eyes on Christ and refuse to pay any attention to those thorns Satan puts in the path. You will be a much stronger man when you come out on the other end victorious.

b. Colossians 3:23: _____

_____

_____

12. Get into the _____ of going to bed _____
and getting up _____.

Again, what do these verses below add to this point?

a. Proverbs 6:9: _____

_____

_____

b. Proverbs 26:14: _____

_____

_____

The way you spend your time truly reflects the passions of your
heart. Are you content with living selfishly by spending the
majority of your time doing absolutely nothing to further God's
kingdom? Or, when you go to bed at night are you full of
excitement for the moment your alarm clock goes off, and you
can begin to discover what the Lord has planned for you for yet
another day? Brother, do not allow your bed to become a
stumbling block for God's great plans for your life. Sleep is just
not worth missing out on such blessings.

13. _____ your _____! _____ your
_____! _____ your _____! And work it
_____. Never, never _____ no matter what
happens.

Note how the following verses add to this final suggestion.

a. I Corinthians 15:58: _____

_____

_____

Jesus Christ desires that you attempt mighty things for His name, but He does not promise a life of ease. Satan will tempt you to quit "wasting your time", the world will tell you to pursue more worthwhile causes, and your flesh will attempt to talk you into taking it easy and settling for simplicity. However, when you choose to follow hard after a life of Godliness your work is never in vain. Each trial and temptation, when overcome, only makes you more like Christ. Ultimately, a life of such devotion is successful in the most meaningful sense of the word.

b. Hebrews 6:12: _____

_____

_____

JUST DO IT

In conclusion to this lesson please read John 17:4. In Jesus' prayer to His Father, He claims that God was glorified as a result of the Son completing the work He was sent to accomplish. Though your purpose is clearly different from that of Jesus Christ, please do not think for a second that it is insignificant. When God created you, He gave you a specific personality with certain talents so that you may be able to successfully accomplish a particular work for His kingdom. It is your responsibility and obligation as a child of God to discover what this work is. You do so by determining your make-up, skills, and passions. Then, you pray diligently for God to reveal His purpose. If you choose to ignore this divine call on your life because you prefer laziness and comfort, please realize you are not the only one affected by such a selfish decision. Rather, those individuals who God purposefully created with the intentions of your influence playing a significant role in their lives, may never come to know of the saving grace of Jesus Christ. Is such a tragedy really worth an extra hour in bed or catching your favorite TV show?

THINGS I WISH SOMEONE HAD TOLD ME WHEN I WAS TWELVE

STUDY SEVENTEEN

"I have learnt that success is to be measured not so much by the position that one has reached in life as by the obstacles which he has overcome while trying to succeed."
—Booker T. Washington

This letter is going to be more of a review than a Bible study. In prior lessons we have already dealt in detail with the majority of the issues mentioned. Thus, be prepared to look back on past letters in order to complete this lesson. As you near the completion of this workbook, it is very beneficial to look back and refresh your memory on some of the topics we have discussed. It would be a shame to work so diligently merely to remain unchanged, weeks later. So, rather than seeing this lesson as busy work or with a "been there, done that" attitude, let us approach it as a way to test our progress thus far.

As the title conveys, this lesson mentions ten truths that could positively impact the life of every young black man. If you will accept this wisdom as a guideline for your life, it is certain that you can avoid much hurt and disappointment. Merely working through this lesson, closing the book, and going on with life just as you please is a waste of time. If that is your intention you may as well choose a more worthwhile way to spend these next few minutes. However, if you are eager to learn from one who has lived longer than you and has learned many of these lessons the hard way, then you are already on the road to success. With that said, let us begin to unravel these ten things.

I. First of all, I wish someone had seriously taken the Bible and plainly showed me what true _____ really meant when I was younger.

1. Can you remember (without looking at lesson 2) what salvation really means? Explain it to the best of your ability below.

_____

_____

_____

_____

Now, turn back to lesson 2 and answer the following questions.

a. The first step in knowing God personally is to understand that you are a _____.

b. What is the punishment for our sin? _____

c. In order to remedy this depressing situation God wants us to understand that He _____ us more than we love _____.

d. Who must you go through in order to really know God?

_____

e. In summation, if you want to know God, the source of all love, joy, peace, real happiness, and true success, _____ in your _____ that Jesus Christ _____, was _____, and _____ again for you. _____ Him to come into your heart and save you. And He will.

140

Is this similar to what you wrote above? If the concept of salvation is still unclear, please diligently review the Scriptures we worked through in lesson 2. Also, do not hesitate to ask your pastor for further explanation. If you are not sure of your own salvation and do not feel qualified enough to explain the plan of salvation with a lost brother you must take care of this. It is truly the most important thing you will ever do.

II. Second, I wish someone had told me about the importance of _____, _____, and _____ the Bible to my life.

Turn to lesson 4 in order to complete the review of this point.

a. What are the three steps to true Bible study mentioned in lesson 4?

1. _____
2. _____
3. _____

Now, reflect on your Bible study habits over the last few weeks. Have you attempted to practice these steps? Has your hunger for God's Word increased?

If so, is it not exciting to finally experience the life-giving power of this Holy Book? If not, you may want to ask yourself why you are putting so much time into this study. Just like James 1:22 says, *"Be ye doers of the word, and not hearers only."* I encourage you to determine to spend quality time in the study of God's Word. Find a place you can be alone and spend some time in prayer preparing your heart for the Lord's presence, and then read from the Bible as though you are expecting to be challenged and changed. Too often we read just so we can mark it off our to-do list or to fulfill someone else's expectations. Try to free yourself from such obligations, and begin to see the reading of God's Word as a precious gift which allows mere human beings to actually interact with the Creator of this universe. Then, before completing your study time, pray for God to help you be a "doer of the Word." Leave that time intentionally looking for opportunities to act upon what you have learned. If you adopt this practice, your intimacy with Jesus Christ will be taken to a level you never imagined possible.

III. Third, I wish someone had forcibly told me to avoid having _____ until after I was _____.

a. We touched on this topic of sexual morality in letter 16. In that lesson we discovered that the Bible clearly lays out specific expectations concerning the way a Christian man deals with the many sexual temptations society throws at him. Re-read Romans 12:1 and I Corinthians 6:18-20 and list every expectation mentioned in these verses.

_____

_____

_____

_____

The Bible does not leave the issue of sex up to interpretation. It clearly says that engaging in sexual activities outside of marriage defiles your body which is to be set apart as the acceptable dwelling place of the Holy Spirit. Now the choice is yours. Will you choose to use your body to honor God or your own fleshly temptations?

IV. Fourth, I wish someone had taught me about the proverbial "_____ of a _____." In other words, I wish someone had taught me how to _____ money better, and how to _____ and _____ it as well.

CHECK IT OUT

a. Please read Matthew 25:14-29 and note how this verse suggests a believer should handle the blessing of wealth.

_____

_____

_____

When you realize that everything you own ultimately belongs to the Lord and is to be used for His purposes, then you will desire to practice incredible responsibility with your wealth. You will find it necessary to learn how to best manage your money, not for your own gain, but in order to partake in the work of God's kingdom. If you prove trustworthy in fulfilling your responsibility with your possessions, then God will be able to trust you with even greater responsibilities.

V. Fifth, I wish that someone had taught me how to _____ my _____ better. Time is like _____ — we must spend it wisely.

Read the following verses and note how they contribute to this point:

a. Psalm 144:4: _____

_____

_____

Every wasted day is incredibly significant. You only have one opportunity to obey the Lord and fulfill His purposes for each minute, hour, day, and week you live. Are you living with such urgency, or are your blessed days just floating by, like a vapor, with no meaningful fruit left behind?

b. Acts 17:24-26: _____

_____

_____

It is up to you to choose whether or not you will acknowledge that you are significant, and you exist for an incredibly specific, exciting purpose. Do not spend another day living with your head down, feeling insignificant, and as though your life has no purpose. Brother, your life is meant to accomplish incredible things HERE and NOW. These words are not my own, they are from the very Word of God.

VI. Sixth, I wish that someone had taught me to have a better _____ _____. There is nothing wrong with _____ work.

a. In lesson 20 we talked about overcoming laziness by accepting hard work. In that lesson you recorded one goal that you hope to accomplish in your life. What was the goal you chose?

_____

b. Have you thought of any other ways you may go about achieving this goal? Please record those below.

_____

_____

_____

Do you really believe you can successfully see this dream come to fruition in your life? I am sure it will take diligent, committed work. Have you resolved to accomplish it no matter what this world throws your way?

VII. Seventh, I wish someone had told me, in a forcible manner, that Junior High School and High School were not times in which to _____, but to _____ _____.

Let us look back at lesson 9 to review this point.

a. What are three of the seven mentioned advantages to increasing your knowledge?

_____

_____

_____

If you are still in school has your attitude toward learning changed over the last few weeks? Are you beginning to treat school as a privilege and not a burden? If you still find yourself dragging your feet to get your homework finished, looking for every possible opportunity to get attention in class, and disrespecting the authority figures in your school, you need to do a major heart check-up. Does it seem you are more devoted to your own reputation and self-image than to Christ being glorified through your life?

VIII. Eighth, I wish someone had told me that life was not going to always be _____, and that I needed to take life more _____ because this is the only life I get.

a. In James 4:14 we see a statement similar to the one we just studied in Psalm 144:4. Read this verse and note what James compares this life to.

_____

b. How is life like a vapor according to this verse?

_____

_____

Not only do we only have one life, but it is a short life. Are you living in such a way that will leave a positive influence even when you leave this earth?

c. Now read Luke 9:23. What command does Jesus give in this verse?

_____

_____

Too often people attempt to persuade others to accept the Christian faith by claiming that it makes life so easy. Friend, according to this verse a follower of Christ should live one of the most difficult lives of anyone. To pick up your cross is to intentionally choose rejection, discomfort, and self-denial so that Christ may be glorified. We were not called to lives of comfort and ease. That is what we have to look forward to in Heaven. Here on earth, you are to expect trials and tribulations. Just think of the heroes in the Bible. Abraham was called to sacrifice his son, Moses never was permitted entrance into the Promised Land, John the Baptist was beheaded, Jesus was crucified, Paul experienced numerous imprisonments, beatings, stonings, and was ultimately martyred, etc. The list could go on and on, but I think you get the picture. Simply being a Christian does not make you immune to tough times; in fact it makes you more vulnerable. However, in the end you are promised peace, comfort, and joy as you stand in the presence of all those names listed above, worshipping God Almighty as one unified body.

IX. Ninth, I wish someone had told me that just because we had integration in our schools, ＿＿＿＿＿＿＿＿ and ＿＿＿＿＿＿＿ did not end.

a. How does Romans 2:9-11 suggest how God might feel about racism?

＿＿＿＿＿＿＿＿＿＿＿＿＿＿＿＿＿＿＿＿＿＿＿＿＿＿＿

＿＿＿＿＿＿＿＿＿＿＿＿＿＿＿＿＿＿＿＿＿＿＿＿＿＿＿

b. What hope does John 16:33 give you for dealing with those times you will encounter prejudice or racism?

＿＿＿＿＿＿＿＿＿＿＿＿＿＿＿＿＿＿＿＿＿＿＿＿＿＿＿

＿＿＿＿＿＿＿＿＿＿＿＿＿＿＿＿＿＿＿＿＿＿＿＿＿＿＿

God clearly opposes racism, not only because it is a sin, but also because His own Son surely experienced the pain that comes from such hatred. Jesus was a Jewish Man living in the pagan Roman society. It is almost certain that He received His share of hurtful comments, bad looks, and societal injustices. However, in this verse Jesus claims victory over all of the forces of this world —

including racism. So, He says, "Cheer up, stand tall, and rest assured your trials do not go unnoticed. I experienced them as well, and I overcame. Thus, by trusting in Me victory is your reward!"

X. Tenth, I wish someone had forcibly told me not to hang around the _____ _____.

In lesson 10 we talked about choosing your friends wisely.

a. If your friends are not increasing in _____,
and if they are not _____ you to do the same,
then you are _____ with the _____ _____.

This statement is not just referring to book knowledge, but even more importantly to the knowledge of God.

Have you taken the time to analyze your friendships? Do the guys you hang out with encourage you to be more like Christ? Do you encourage them in the same way? If not, why are you waiting to take action and seek out Godly friends? Sure, it is not easy to drop the only friends you have ever known, but if it is the right thing to do then you must be obedient. Remember, life is not about ease, it is about bringing glory to God. You only have one life to live and the length of it is unknown. Thus, I encourage you not to waste another day living for yourself. Rather, invest in a cause that is eternal — Jesus Christ.

You have worked very hard today, so we are not going to do a final exercise. I hope this review has helped you to see if your reading of this book has been worthwhile thus far.

JUST DO IT

If you are still dragging your feet, waiting until another day to make changes in your life, let me just warn you that such an attitude usually results in no change — ever. If the Holy Spirit has convicted you about any of the issues discussed, determine to begin going down the right path TODAY.

HOW TO BE REALLY COOL

STUDY EIGHTEEN

"The secret of success is to be like a duck — smooth and unruffled on top, but paddling furiously underneath."
—Unknown

This is going to be a rather short lesson. For one, you worked very hard in the past lesson and deserve a break. Also, letter 22 is shorter in length. The real question ultimately becomes whether you desire to be cool according to the world's standards or according to God's expectations.

1. List five examples of things that are not cool according to the book:

A. _____

B. _____

C. _____

D. _____

E. _____

2. What else can you add to this list that the world seems to claim is really cool, but in reality it is far from pleasing to God?

_____

_____

_____

3. So, what is real coolness according to the book?

A. Real coolness is being _____ so that you will never look un-cool.

B. Real coolness is being _____ at the various vicissitudes of life.

C. Real coolness is that _____ _____ in knowing that God is in _____ and knowing that everything will be alright.

D. Coolness is having inexplicable _____, _____ and _____ even in the midst of the storms of life.

E. Being cool is also being able to _____ yourself _____ even when you are under fire.

F. Being cool is being able to keep your _____ under _____ even when defending yourself from the accusations of fools.

4. I would like to add just one key characteristic to being cool. So often we picture cool people as those who receive a lot of attention, those who tend to be popular, and those who seem to be everywhere and in the middle of everything. They usually influence others by what they say, wear, and do. This world likes to place cool people on a pedestal so that all may pay their respects. However, the Bible's idea of one worthy of honor and attention is quite the opposite.

Read the following verses and note how they directly oppose this world's understanding of coolness.

a. Matthew 20:16: _____

_____

_____

b. Mark 9:35: _____

_____

_____

Those who this world tends to place in the shadows are the ones who will stand in the light in the end. People who constantly seek after attention and popularity had better enjoy it while they can because come eternity, their time in the spotlight will be long gone. On the other hand, the individual who serves the Lord quietly and with integrity will be rewarded. The young man who chooses to respect his teacher and classmates rather than be a distraction in the classroom pleases the Lord. The individual who does not flaunt his talents and brag so that all will pay him recognition, but rather humbly accepts his skills as blessings from the Lord to be used for kingdom purposes, is highly favored in God's eyes. If you desire to ever be on top, you must first be humble enough to be on the bottom.

Friend, if you are already consider yourself to be a cool individual I encourage you to determine whether or not your reputation is more important to you than God's will. Now, do not get me wrong. Being cool is not a bad thing. In fact, those who are respected among their peers have the greatest opportunity to positively effect an entire generation. However, if it is possible that your reputation has become more important to you than serving God, then you will need to re-examine your priorities. Remember, if you choose to be cool in the eyes of this world, no matter what the cost, then the praise you receive from man is your reward in full. Enjoy every minute of it while on this earth, for it will surely cease when this life is over. However, if you truly desire to please God above man, you will be eager to make yourself less so that He can be made greater. In reality, what does this dark, hurting, dying world need more — you or Jesus Christ?

JUST DO IT

In conclusion, I encourage you to do all you can to be a cool individual. By this, I am of course referring to the Lord's standards for coolness, not those of this world.

WOMEN FOLK!

STUDY NINETEEN

"God save us from wives who are angels in the street, saints in the church, and devils at home."

—Spurgeon

In this study, we will look at one of the most important, issues for young black men, or any man, for that matter, and that is your relationship with the women folk.

1. A _____ woman can _____ you become a _____ _____ in life; a _____ woman can not only _____ _____ _____ _____, but she can _____ your life as well.

CHECK IT OUT

Read the following verses and note what they say about the good and the bad woman:

a. Proverbs 12:4: _____

_____

_____

b. Proverbs 23:27-28: _____

_____

_____

There are two kinds of women in this world: one is the good woman who will build you up and the other is the bad woman who can tear you down.

2. Understand that women are _____ by _____ to be a _____ and a _____ to man, _____ a _____.

3. Don't let your life be _____ by _____, but rather by _____ _____ and _____ _____ _____.

Note what these verses says regarding this subject:

a. I Corinthians 6:18: _____
_____
_____

b. I Corinthians 6:15: _____
_____
_____

4. Most pretty and fine women are _____ _____ _____ _____.

a. Learn quickly to get _____ the _____ and _____ _____ about the _____.

b. What you want, son, and what you had better get in a woman, is a woman of _____, _____,

_____, and _____.

c. If you fool around and get yourself a woman who is beautiful on the outside, yet on the inside she is full of lies, cheating, rebellion, stubbornness, disrespect, manipulation, etc., etc.,

_____ _____ _____ _____ _____

_____.

5. Notice these verses from the Word of God:

a. Proverbs 31:10-31: _____

_____

_____

b. Titus 2:3-5: _____

_____

_____

c. I Peter 3:1-2: _____

_____

_____

6. As you are in the process of looking for that special someone, please _____ _____ _____ and the _____ for the _____ _____ _____.

7. Don't be _____ of women nor be _____ by women.

157

8. You are _____ _____ too.

9. Women _____ men just as much as men _____ women.

10. _____ women like _____ men.

11. According to the book, what are five of the eleven characteristics that women like to see in men:

a. _____

b. _____

c. _____

d. _____

e. _____

12. Understand, son, that _____ _____ _____ to be the _____ of the relationship.

a. Lovingly _____ that your relationship be this way because _____ _____ for it to be this way.

b. If you are a _____, _____ leader, a "good woman" will _____ _____, at all, lining up with your leadership.

c. Good, decent women _____ strong, loving, _____ male _____, and they _____ or will eventually despise a man who is not a strong leader and who lets her control him and manipulate him.

d. Be a strong, loving man who knows where he is _____, knows what he _____, who can _____ _____, and who does not allow women to _____ him.

13. _____ for a _____ woman and _____ _____.

If you pray and seek the Lord's guidance, and follow the advice above, I guarantee you that you will have a happy and successful relationship with the woman in your life.

JUST DO IT

Read the following verses on the man's role as well as the woman's role, and pray and ask God to help you to be the strong, Christian man that He wants you to be; and, also pray and ask God to bless you with the woman that he wants you to have, and that will be a great help-meet for you.

    1. Ephesians 5:22-33
    2. Colossians 3:18-19
    3. Titus 2:1-8
    4. I Peter 3:1-7

THINK FOR YOURSELF!

STUDY TWENTY

"The ultimate measure of a man is not where he stands in moments of comfort and convenience, but where he stands at times of challenge and controversy."
— Dr. Martin Luther King, Jr.

It is very appropriate to finish this study with a lesson on leadership. If you have resolved to live for Jesus Christ in every aspect of your life, then you must also choose to be a leader. Our society needs strong, influential, Christian men and women to stand up if this world is ever going to leave its path of destruction and accept Christ's command to follow Him. Clearly, thinking for yourself is one of the primary ways to set yourself apart from the crowd. Too many individuals believe everything they are told in school, on television, in the newspaper, and by other influential people. Sometimes this is okay, but it often leads to deception and beliefs that simply do not line up with the Bible. Thus, in this lesson we will quickly review the ways you should think for yourself, and then we will do a closer study on leadership. At the conclusion of this lesson you will surely be equipped to overcome mundane, insignificant living and take on a life of commitment, devotion, and great influence.

1. Be a _____ instead of a _____.
We have _____ followers. Think for _____. Be the leader that _____ _____ you to be.

In order to learn how to think for yourself, you need to do at least three things:

A. You need to _____ up every _____ and his
   _____ with the rule book: the _____.

B. You need to have a set of _____ about the
   issues of life based upon a _____ foundation.

C. You need to _____ what people say before you
   _____ it "hook, line, and sinker," so to speak.

Take these three suggestions to heart and put them into practice
so you will not be deceived by the many, many lies in our society.

Thinking for yourself is certainly one mark of being a leader.
However, there are many areas in which you should stand apart
and exhibit influence as a Christian. So, let us open our Bibles
and see what it has to say concerning leadership.

CHECK IT OUT

2. Read Matthew 5:14. According to this verse, what is your role
as a believer?

_____

_____

In order to be light you must be willing to position yourself in
places of darkness and intentionally stand out. In a world of
hopelessness, you are to bring the message of hope. In a world of
suffering, you are to claim the promise of a future kingdom in
which tears and pain do not exist. In a world of injustice, you are
to speak up for what is right. In a world of poverty, you are to
care for the orphans and widows and proclaim the true treasure
which is in heaven. If you choose to merely blend into the

darkness, you will be just another individual consumed by this dry, barren land. However, if you gladly take on this role of being the light, others will constantly be drawn to your life and message — which will ultimately lead them to the true source of light, Jesus Christ. Brother, accept this call to be a leader, to stand above the crowd, and to turn other's eyes toward heaven.

3. Please read 1 Timothy 4:12. According to the first part of the verse, what characteristic is not to be used as an excuse for following rather than leading?

_____

_____

4. In which five areas are you to set an example of those who follow Jesus Christ?

_____

_____

_____

_____

_____

We are going to look at each of these in a little more detail.

First, let us see how God expects Christians to stand apart in their speech.

What do the following verses say about how a believer should and should not use his tongue?

5. 1 Peter 3:9-10: _____

_____

_____

6. James 1:26: _____

_____

_____

Your tongue is a direct reflection of what is in your heart. In a split second you can use your tongue to ruin another's reputation, hurt a loved one's feelings, use the Father's name in vain, etc. Likewise, this same vessel can be used to sing praise to God, tell a lost friend of His goodness, and encourage a down and out brother. You are the only one who controls the purposes for which your tongue will be used. Be slow to talk and quick to listen. Think before you speak, so that you might use your speech to glorify God rather than hurt your peers.

Next, let us see what the Bible has to say about setting an example through your life or conduct.

How do these verses encourage a Christian to conduct himself?

7. John 13:12-15: _____

_____

_____

As a leader, you are to conduct yourself as a servant. This may seem a bit backwards, but people will be much more drawn to those who care for their needs and demonstrate compassion. Live your life in such a manner that you are quick to meet the needs of others and slow to expect your own needs to be met.

8. Titus 2:7-8: _____

_____

_____

As a Christian you are also expected to set an example in love. Now this is not the same kind of sensual, passionate love the world is so obsessed with. Rather, in 1 Timothy 4, Paul is talking about true, genuine love. To understand what characteristics comprise such love, read a section from a different letter of Paul.

9. Read 1 Corinthians 13 and record every characteristic of love mentioned.

_____

_____

_____

_____

_____

_____

_____

_____

_____

_____

_____

_____

_____

Imagine an individual who actually epitomized every description above. Would others not flock to be in his presence and treat him with the utmost respect? Such an individual would have great influence because he cared for others more than himself. Brother, this description of one who truly possesses love is not hypothetical. Rather, it is an attainable expectancy for all believers. As a Christian, the very spirit of God resides in your heart. If you allow Him to take control, you will be the influential leader you imagined. It all starts by making yourself less, so Christ may be more.

Moving on, 1 Timothy 4:12 also calls you to set an example in faith.

Read Colossians 2:5-10 and note how you go about possessing an influential faith.

10. First, according to verse 5 your faith must be in _____ and it must be accompanied by _____.

11. What is the commandment given in verse 6? _____
_____

According to verse 7 your faith needs to be firmly rooted and established in Christ Jesus.

12. If you practice all of these commands given in verses 5-7, you will be prepared to overcome the obstacles mentioned in verse 8. What are these obstacles?

_____
_____
_____

13. According to verse 10, who is the head and authority over all? Circle one.

   (A) The Church
   (B) The Educated
   (C) The Government
   (D) The Son of God

Your faith should be one that is unchanging and uninfluenced by the trends of this world. You have believed in the One and Only God whose ways are much higher than man's ways. In order to walk in Christ you must be disciplined enough to study, remember, and apply His Word to your life. If you do not know the promises and truths contained in the Bible, you will be vulnerable to the philosophical, deceitful attacks that this world throws your way. As a leader, you must know what you believe and why you believe it. Simply saying that Christianity is the religion of your mother and grandmother will not suffice. Think for yourself. Delve into the doctrines of this faith and become well-grounded in the truth. This world will be much more willing to follow a man who claims the authority of God Almighty above that of his mother or grandmother.

Finally, you must set an example of believers by your purity. We have already talked a lot about purity throughout this study. Just for a quick refresher, read the following verse and note what it means to live a life of purity.

14. 2 Timothy 2:22: _____
_____
_____

In order to call on the name of the holy Lord, you should have a pure heart. According to this verse, such purity comes from fleeing youthful lusts and intentionally pursuing righteousness. Remember, from our first weeks together, that righteousness is synonymous to an absence of sin. You are also to pursue faith, love, and peace. Are such passions reflections of your heart? Do you consistently flee the temptations that lead to defilement, and seek after a life worthy of the calling of Jesus Christ? As a leader, you are to stand apart in this area. When your peers obsess over things which are sexual, you should stand apart and obsess over that which is Godly. It may be awkward to stick out, but such is the fate of those who choose to be the light amidst a dark world.

You have worked diligently throughout this entire study. Such commitment does not go unnoticed by God. He is thrilled that you are stepping up to the plate, making a conscious decision to live a life much bigger than yourself. God cannot wait to use you for mighty purposes. However, He will likely begin testing your faith and obedience in small ways. Stay strong, brother. If you are serious about pursuing a life of Godliness, be certain that the devil will step up his attacks on you. Do not believe his lies and do not be discouraged. You are already on the winning team. Claim that victory, and live a life of confidence. You have no idea what a huge difference you will make in your family, amongst your peers, in your community, and ultimately in the whole world.

I would like to conclude with my personal prayer for each young man who has read the book and worked diligently through this study. My prayer for you is found in Philippians 1:9-11. I pray that this might be your prayer for your own life as well.

"And this I pray, that your love may abound yet more and more in knowledge and in all judgement; That ye may approve

things that are excellent; that ye may be sincere and without offence till the day of Christ; Being filled with the fruits of righteousness, which are by Jesus Christ, unto the glory and praise of God."

JUST DO IT

GO OUT AND BE A GODLY LEADER, YBM!

"PRAY! THINK! DO!"
—Daniel Whyte III

ANSWERS

Study One: *The Main Thing*

1. body, spirit
2.-7. Answers may vary
8. relationship with God
9. health, wealth, education
10.-19. Answers may vary.

Study Two: *Get to Know Your Creator*

I. personally, yourself
   a. sinner
   b. unrighteousness
   c.-f. Answers may vary
II. sin, punishment, death, spiritual, physical
   a.-c. Answers may vary
III.
   a. loves, ourselves
   b. Answers may vary
IV. His only begotten Son, Jesus Christ
   a.-c. Answers may vary
V. love, joy, peace, happiness, success, heart, died, buried, rose, you

Study Three: *How to Obtain the Blessings of God*

1. happy, successful
2. Answers may vary
3. attitude, parents
4.-6. Answers may vary
7. blessings, choose, obedient
8. obedience, not, disobedience, never, never
9.-11. Answers may vary
12. prayer, blessings
13.-15. Answers may vary
16. blessed, faith
17.-20. Answers may vary
21. stronger, dynamic, reading the Bible

22. giving

23.-24. Answers may vary

25. a. Have the right attitude toward your parents; b. Be obedient to God's Word; c. Spend quality time in prayer; d. Have faith in God; e. Get into the habit of giving

Study Four: *Your Road Map to Real and Lasting Success*

1. successful, read, meditate, obey, Bible, success

2. success, God's Word, daily

3.-4. Answers may vary

5. A. Pray, praying, spiritual, Holy Spirit

6.-7. Answers may vary

B. retain, think upon, remember

8.-9. Answers may vary

C. obey, hearer, doer

10.-11. Answers may vary

12. *It will make you wise; It will give you direction in life; It will strengthen, fortify, and stabilize you; It will help you help others; It will make you genuinely successful.*

13. Answers may vary

Study Five: *Tap Into Unlimited Power*

1. Answers may vary

2. power

3. God, prayer, in, through, for

4. -7. Answers may vary

8. experience, changes

9.-16. Answers may vary

17. a. praise; b. will; c. daily provisions; d. forgiveness; e. evil; f. glory

18. everything, heart, mind, enjoy

19.-21. Answers may vary

Study Six: *The Encouragement Place*

1. close, church

2. ought to be involved in a good church
    I. God wants
        A. Answers may vary

B. Answers may vary

III. regularly, strengthen, build, preaching, teaching

C. Answers may vary

III. opportunity, privilege, worship, serve

D. Answers may vary

E. Answers may vary

IV. joy, privilege, exhort

F. To urge and encourage to keep going on strong for God.

G. Answers may vary

H. Answers may vary

I. 1. A pastor that truly is a born-again Christian; 2. Preaching and teaching from the Bible as it is written; 3. A pastor and church that believe the essentials of the Christian faith; 4. A church that carries out the Great Commission; 5. The leaders and people strive to live according to the Bible.

J. 1. right attitude, 2. humble spirit, 3. praying heart, 4. worship God, glory

Study Seven: *Pulling Others Out of the Fire*

1. blessed, blessings
2. freely, received, give
3. Answers may vary
4. Answers may vary
5. light, knowledge, you, God, our people
6. through social programs alone; through education alone; through the government alone
7. God, principles, His Word
8.-12. Answers may vary
13. root problem, SIN, Jesus Christ, God's plan of salvation
14. A. Show them from God's Word that "We are all sinners"; B. Show them that there is a great punishment for sin, that is, eternal separation from God in a place called hell; C. Show them that inspite of their sin, God still loves them and wants to save them; D. Show them that all they have to do to be saved is trust in Jesus Christ.

Study Eight: *The Awesome Value of Reading & The Importance of Increasing Knowledge*

    1.-3. Answers may vary
    4. increasing your knowledge
    5.-7. Answers may vary
    8. Seven advantages of increasing your knowledge inside the book
    9. CHANGE YOUR ATTITUDE TOWARD EDUCATION AND KNOWLEDGE!; play; partying; foolishness; serious business
    10. "by any means necessary"
    11. Answers may vary

Study Nine: *The Obstacles to Getting A Good Education & Graduating From College and Still Ignorant and Unlearned*

    I. yourself
        A. made up mind, will, discipline
        B. Answers may vary
        C. Answers may vary
    II. immediate money, gratification
        A. Answers may vary
        B. Answers may vary
    III. be your friends
        A. knowledge, exhorting, are flying with the wrong birds
        B. Answers may vary
        C. Answers may vary
        D. Answers may vary
    IV. finding the right college
        A. Answers may vary
        B. Answers may vary
        C. Answers may vary
    V. money
        A. Answers may vary
        B. Answers may vary
        C. good education
    1. wrong idea, learning anything
        A. Answers may vary
        B. Answers may vary

Study Ten: *The Marks of a Truly Educated Man & Please Learn "Yourself"
A Little Etiquette*

    1. healthy, humble respect, reverence
        a. not, wise, educated, fool
        b.-e. Answers may vary
    2. humble enough to admit his ignorance
        a.-c. Answers may vary
    3. continues, education
        a. grows, goes
    4. authentic
        a.-c. Answers may vary
    5. wise, good purposes
        a. Answers may vary
        b. Answers may vary
    6. ability to express himself clearly through his speech and through his writing
    7. disciplined
        a. when he does not feel like doing them
        b. Answers may vary
        c. Answers may vary
    8. quiet confidence
        a. Answers may vary
        b. Answers may vary
    9. strives, moral man
        a. right thing
        b. Answers may vary
        c. Answers may vary
    10. etiquette, protocol
        a. relates to other people
        b. Answers may vary
        c. right, proper, polite, kind, fellow human beings

Study Eleven: *With All Thy Getting, Get Wisdom & Understanding*

    1. wisdom
    2. Wisdom is having skill. Wisdom tells you why you ought to do something and when you should do it.
    3.   a.-h. Answers may vary

j. pure, peaceable, gentle, easy to be intreated, full of mercy and good fruits, without partiality, without hypocrisy
4. the fear of the Lord
5. Answers may vary
6. ASK GOD FOR IT!
7. work, study, borrow, buy, extract
   a.-b. Answers may vary
8. walk, hang, wise men, fool yourself
   a. Answers may vary

Study Twelve: *You Are Not Inferior!*

I. not, raised right
   a. love, nurturing, encouragement, black boys, crucial
   b. Answers may vary
II. addicted, television set
   a. others, doing, progressing, moving forward, watch
   b. Answers may vary
III. pursue, knowledge
   a. POWER, huge power
   b.-d. Answers may vary
1. a.-c. Answers may vary
2. a.-b. Answers may vary
3. a.-c. Answers may vary

Study Thirteen: *Take the Road Less Traveled*

1. The tough, lonely road of self-discipline
2. determined, task done, reach, goal, feel, going on, willing, sacrifice, without
3. prayer, reading, in-depth study, exercise, sex
4.   a. feel, don't
      b. Answers may vary
5. Bible
      a. the Sword of the Spirit
      b. Answers may vary
6.   a. Answers may vary
7.   a. -c. Answers may vary
8. -10. Answers may vary

Study Fourteen: *Take Full Responsibility & Talk and Listen to Every Older Black Man Past Fifty that you Possibly Can*

1. not, healthy, responsibilty, afraid, handicap
    a. Answers may vary
2. We have never been taught it, and we have not seen it exemplified by many older black men.
    a. Answers may vary
3. Answers may vary
4. Answers may vary
5. self-responsibility, against human nature
    a. easier, irresponsible, responsible
    b. Answers may vary
    c. Answers may vary
6. A. You will live a sad life constantly having to blame others for your failures and problems; B. You will live a life of constantly being a follower and not a leader; C. You will live a life of constantly depending on other people.
7. By simply making a firm resolute DECISION to be responsible for yourself, your life, and for those God places under your care.
8. responsibility, all, do, say, are, blame
9. quality time talking, listening, older black man
10. Possible answers are in book
11. He is in the temple listening to the teachers and asking questions.
12. He was equipped to call others to follow him, to teach in spiritual settings, and to heal the sick in the name of God.
13. Simply, they came to Jesus.
14. Jesus is teaching while the disciples are listening.
15. Jesus sends the disciples out to rescue His lost sheep and to preach about the kingdom of Heaven. They are to perform miracles and healings.

Study Fifteen: *Learn About Where You Come From*

1. self-esteem, confidence, future, where he came from, where he is going
2.   A. visit, older relatives
        B. Black American history
        C. Africa

D. American history

3. The night the Lord spared His chosen people who marked their doorways with the blood of a sacrificial lamb.

4. God had set apart His people in a very intimate way, and He displayed His faithfulness in this act of protection.

5. He brought them out of Egypt, thus freeing them from their oppressors and chains.

6. Do not be afraid. Stand firm and you will see the deliverance the Lord will bring today.

7. Moses lifted up his hand and the Lord parted the Red Sea back so the Israelites could cross on dry land.

8. The Lord is fighting for the Israelites. Let us get away from them!

9. The Egyptians were swept into the sea, without leaving a single survivor behind. The Israelites, on the other hand, went straight through the sea with a wall of water on each side.

10. The Lord protected His precious children who trusted Him and obeyed His commands.

11. To preserve some of the manna in a jar and keep it for future generations.

12. God wanted the future generations to see how He provided for their ancestors in their time of greatest need.

13. As long as Moses held up his hands, the Israelites were winning.

14. Joshua overcame the Amalekite army with the sword. The Israelites were victorious.

15. He commands that Moses write down these events on a scroll as something to be remembered.

16. Israel was to obey Him fully and keep His covenant. They were to be a holy nation, set apart for holy purposes.

17. Because the Israelites continued to treat Him with contempt and refused to believe in spite of the many miraculous signs He performed.

18. Not one of the men who witnessed the miraculous signs of the Lord and still disobeyed His commandments would enter the Promised Land.

Study Sixteen: *The Value of Working Hard and Smart*

1. lazy, slothful, poor, dependent, work diligently, need, good, desire

2.-5. Answers may vary

6. A. It is a natural tendency of mankind to avoid work and that which is difficult; B. Many young men today are raised to be lazy; C. Many young men become lazy because of their addiction to television and this new thing called the video game.

7. fiction, non-fiction, TV, reality

8. accomplish, specific goals, pursue

9.   a. -d. Answers may vary

10. time schedule, plan, achieve, mad man

    a.-b. Answers may vary

11. determined, anyone, anything, know, ought to do

    a.-b. Answers may vary

12. habit, earlier, earlier

    a.-b. Answers may vary

13. work, plan, work, plan, work, plan, daily, quit

    a.-b. Answers may vary

Study Seventeen: *Things I Wish Someone Had Told Me When I Was Twelve*

I. salvation

    1. Answers may vary

        a. sinner

        b. death

        c. loves, ourselves

        d. Jesus Christ

        e. believe, heart, died, buried, rose, Ask

II. reading, studying, applying

    a. pray then read, read and retain, read and obey

III. sex, married

    a. Answers may vary

IV. value, dollar, manage, save, invest

    a. Answers may vary

V. manage, time, money

    a. Answers may vary

    b. Answers may vary

VI. work ethic, hard

    a. Answers may vary

    b. Answers may vary

VII. play, gain knowledge

    a. Answers may vary

VIII. easy, seriously

    a. He calls it a vapor

b. It appears for a little while and then fades away.

c. Those who desire to follow Jesus must deny themselves, take up their crosses daily, and follow Him.

IX. racism, prejudice

    a. Answers may vary

    b. Answers may vary

X. wrong crowd

    a. knowledge, exhorting, flying, wrong birds

Study Eighteen: *How to be Really Cool*

1. Answers may vary
2. Answers may vary
3.   A. prepared

    B. un-ruffled

    C. quiet confidence, control

    D. peace joy, calmness

    E. express, clearly

    F. tongue, control

4. a.-b. Answers may vary

Study Nineteen: *Women Folk!*

1. good, help, great success, bad, make your life miserable, ruin

    a. -b. Answers may vary

2. designed, God, help, blessing, not, hinderance
3. driven, sex, God's Word, what is right

    a.-b. Answers may vary

4. not good for you

    a. past, exterior, find out, interior

    b. virtue, integrity, trustworthiness, honor

    c. you will have hell to pay

5.   a.-c. Answers may vary
6. put God first, search, right lady second
7. afraid, intimidated
8. the prize
9. desire, desire
10. good, real
11. Answers may vary
12. God made you, leader

    a. insist, God intended

    b. strong, loving, not mind

    c. appreciate, decisive, leadership, despise

    d. going, wants, think independently, hinder

13. pray, good, marry young

Study Twenty: *Think for Yourself!*

  1. leader, follower, enough, yourself, God wants

    A. size, leader, statements, Bible

    B. convictions, biblical

    C. examine, accept

2. To be the light of the world.

3. Being young.

4. Speech, Life, Love, Faith, Purity

5.-8. Answers may vary

9. patience, kind, does not envy, does not brag, is not puffed up, does not act rudely, does not seek its own, is not easily provoked, does not think evil, does not rejoice in iniquity, rejoices in the truth, bears all things, believes all things, hopes all things, endures all things, does not fail

10. Christ, stedfastness

11. Walk in Christ

12. Philosophy and vain deceit, after the tradition of man, after the rudiments of the world, and not after Christ

13. The Son of God

14. Answers may vary